DEFINE & DEFY

UNLEASHING YOUR INNER POTENTIAL

SIM SANDHU & ANGIE CHIK

ISBN: 978-1-928155-60-7

PUBLISHED BY:
AUTHORITY PRESS
MARKHAM, ON
CANADA

Contents

This book is dedicated to our families, first and foremost, for supporting us through our journey, and to Brian Tracy, our friends, and colleagues, who continue to inspire and motivate us to new heights. To the individuals that we will meet down the road when our destinies cross paths, when we make an indelible impression on each other's lives, we dedicate this book to you.

Thousands of candles can be lighted from a single candle,
and the life of the candle will not be shortened.
Happiness never decreases by being shared.

~ Buddha

Foreword

Perhaps the greatest discovery of my life was that each person has enormous reserves of untapped potential that they habitually fail to use. When I came across this finding at the age of 21, it changed my life forever. From that day until this, I have searched for the ideas, insights, messages, secrets and discoveries that enable a person to accomplish more than they ever dreamed possible, no matter where they started out.

Now, in this wonderful book, *Define & Defy*, you will have the great pleasure and delight of learning some of the best ideas and insights ever discovered to help you to become everything you are capable of becoming. With what you learn in this book, you will be able to achieve greater goals, faster than ever before. You will learn how to dream big dreams, and to create a wonderful vision for your life and your future. You will develop the qualities of tenacity and persistence that virtually guarantee you success in the long run.

Sim and Angie have done a wonderful job in researching these key ideas, and then practicing them in their own lives, for months and years, to prove and demonstrate that these are not theoretical or philosophical ideas, but tried and true, practical, proven methods and techniques that really work in the crucible of human experience.

Perhaps the most important thing I learned in the development of human potential is the necessity for you to take action when you come across an idea that you think can be helpful to you. As you read this book, you should make mental notes about the actions that you are going to take as soon as you close these pages. The faster you act, the more likely it is that you will take more and more actions, and make all of your dreams come true.

Congratulations on your decision to embark on this wonderful adventure. Sim and Angie will walk with you, hand in hand, through the pages of this book to enable you to achieve extraordinary things. Good luck!

Brian Tracy
Solana Beach, CA 2015

Introduction
Touching the Skies

We never know how high we are
Till we are called to rise;
And then, if we are true to plan,
Our statures touch the skies.

- Emily Dickinson

Once upon a time, there were two little girls growing up in British Columbia. One grew up playing with toy cars, rolling in the mud, and playing the Indian drums. The other grew up shy and quiet, excelling at drawing, playing the piano and making art out of found objects.

One found herself in an abusive relationship when she was in her early 20s while the other took the conventional path of going into university. Life took them on a little ways. One decided to study criminology and mental health studies and the other immersed herself in studying the brain and the science of behaviour. When they decided to explore the world, one went to Africa and the other ventured into a new province to further her French studies.

However, their stars brought them together and a special bond was created.

Who Are We?

We are the CEOs of Sandhu & Chik Group of Companies. Our businesses are the product of our visioning, our motivation and our hard work, and they hold our interest in everything from transportation to real estate investing to empowerment of individuals through motivational writing and speaking.

Here's the thing about us: We're strong women on our own but, when we met, we knew that we would be completely amazing together as partners in business. Women often are. When you have other strong women around you, confident, ambitious and ready to succeed, there's nothing you can't do, and that's the world that we chose to live in. We decided to sculpt the world to our terms, not have the world shape us on its terms.

Now at the helm of our successful companies, we have joined forces with 6 successful women around the globe to share personal anecdotes of challenges and achievements with ambitious individuals like you. From stories of beating the bullet from a machine gun, to bankruptcy, to stepping out of domestic violence, to running multi-million dollar companies, our main goal in sharing these stories is to empower you to find your true vocation and inner potential to reach for your own successes. We hope these stories will remind you that you are not alone in walking your path and that there are many successful women who have gone through their own trials by fire and come out stronger than before and even more in love with life. You can find their narratives under Success Story from the Frontlines at the end of Chapters 1,2,4,6, 8 and 9.

The word 'success' comes with a spectrum of definitions, unique to each person. Success, to us, means to attain that which you have envisioned and worked hard to achieve, and to learn from the accumulation of life experiences, be they failures or victories. Everything that happens in your life encompasses who you are as an individual. There are many ways to achieve success but, in order for you to reach your true potential in life, you must start with defining who you are and what drives your inner desires based on your temperament and various experiences and lessons you go through. Your passions, goals and vocation are at the intrapersonal level and it is from this level that we derive much of the meaning behind our existence. From then on, once you have a good grasp and understanding of who you are—which may take some individuals a lifetime to discover— you move on to the next level, which is the interpersonal level. How you fit into the community, or how you see yourself in society, and what kind of mark you want to leave in this world is related to how you challenge and defy the status quo and what society deems to be normal and possible. You must consciously decide that no matter how big the challenges are on your road to success—and there will be many, many bumps on your journey—you will defy anything that comes in your way.

Who is this book for? If you've yearned for change to a more fulfilling and meaningful life, this book is for you. If you have had more than your share of frustrations and failures and are ready to claim your place under the sun, this book is also for you.

If you've longed to step into your own greatness, but don't know how, this book is definitely for you. If you are looking for guidance into leading a purposeful and joyful life, one in which you thrive, use this book as your roadmap to living your biggest dreams.

We're ready, we're so, so ready for women who are ready to shake things up. You can run a company, you can claim wealth and success, and more than just deserving it, you can take ownership of what you've envisioned for yourself!

We're entrepreneurs and we are proud to have created our own stories of success. So can you.

The possibilities are endless when you dare to dream, and when you dare to begin your path to action. If you are now ready to change your world, let's begin.

It first begins with understanding who you are.

Chapter 1
I Am Who I Am

Life is not easy for any of us. But what of that? We must have
perseverance and above all confidence in ourselves. We must believe
that we are gifted for something and that this thing must be attained.
– Marie Curie

We are products of our pasts, not prisoners of it.

We are who we are, and we've never succumbed to the status quo. On our own at first, and then slowly and with greater confidence, we found that we were far stronger together than we ever could be apart. We were powerful in ways that we had never dreamed, and we hope that, through the inspiration that we found in each other, we can empower and motivate you in ways that you can't imagine.

There has never been a time like the present for women to rise and to take their places as equals in the world. As of 2014, women represent just 4.8% of the Fortune 500 CEO positions and 5.1% of the Fortune 1000 CEO positions. While this does not seem like a lot, these numbers have doubled since 2011. We can feel that the star of the woman entrepreneur is on the rise, and with this power behind you, it's time to learn what you can do.

Our pasts give us strength but we've never been ones to let our pasts define us. We are who we are, and it wasn't as if we were different people in the past. We've always been ourselves, but time has brought our strengths into focus.

Although our pasts challenged us to overcome painful moments during trying times, pain does not make us strong. All pain does is hurt us. What makes us strong is what we decide to do with that pain. When we tell you our stories, we are not looking for pity or praise. We do not show off our scars because they are exotic or because we think that they make us noble.

Instead, we offer our scars and our stories as maps, a way out of the darkness for some women who were (and are!) living with the things that we have lived with. We want to show you that there is a way not only out, but up. We struggled to find our way in life at first, but when we looked within ourselves and realized what truly encompassed who we are as individuals, we found our direction and carved a path to take us to what mattered most to us in life.

Women Standing United

Here's the thing about lionesses: They hunt in packs. Alone they're still fantastic hunters on their own, together, they're unstoppable. When we joined forces as business partners, we learned immediately there is tremendous strength in numbers. Life is a challenge and, when we met, we instinctively knew that we would be allies, friends, and partners in crime! We knew we wanted to provide a fresh, female perspective to entrepreneurship and to business building.

It is hard to find a business partner you can trust and resonate with. But what works really well in our partnership is that we have pertinent traits and values in common but we couldn't be more different in so many respects. We are both tenacious and strong-willed and, once we set our sights on a target, nothing holds us back.

Sim is bold, confident and freely expresses her feelings. Angie is an analytical thinker and an efficient multi-tasker. Angie loves the complexity of details while Sim is the big picture visionary, who thinks on a global scale. We draw power from our similarities and our individual strengths because we understand that a rich partnership cannot be held back by frail egos and the incessant insistence to be right.

When we started our first business venture together, we knew that we might have to struggle to break the new ground we set our focus on. We knew that there were going to be days when we wanted to quit, and days when our clients made us want to scream. Instead of falling down, we rolled with the punches and came up grinning and ready for more. We were never going to let the business get the better of us. We knew it was never going to be a straight path and we would have to zig and zag and tweak. When the going got rough, we made time to reflect and to course-correct, to re-infuse our lives with meaningful and fulfilling activities.

What we want to tell you is that, as women, we have a deep and enduring strength that can't be beaten. When we met each other, we recognized something – a grittiness in each other. We saw guts and courage and an unquenchable desire to live to peak potential, yet we also saw compassion, empathy and a determination to do good in the world.

There is a saying that women always have to compete with each other. Whether it is for romance, for resources, for money or for jobs, the movies and the books tell us that two women in one place is always bad news.

That's old and outdated rhetoric. In our world, there is a culture of collaboration, not competition. We are all about inclusion, consultation and cohesion through shared values. We believe in passion, performance, inspiration and creativity. Our method of doing business and our values have led us to success, and as we continue to grow and push ourselves out of our comfort zone, challenges that arise become more invigorating and galvanizing! Life is essentially about living your dreams and passions and bettering yourself each day. We want you to know that you shouldn't allow fear and intimidation stop you from pursuing your dreams and from ultimately and inevitably reaching your success!

Ambitious?
Yes.

Bold?
Yes.

Fearless?
Yes, yes and yes!

We're here in spite of what we have gone through, and throughout the storm and the trials of our lives, we have stood firm, and now we stand united.

Let us lead you along the path, and let us show you where we have been, if only to make it a little easier for you to relate. We are who we are, not in spite of our pasts, not because we decided to play victim, not because we chose to play safe and settle for convention. We are who we are because our pasts challenged us and tested us and convinced us there is a better, freer way to live our lives and to make a difference in the world.

The Joys of Tabla and the Darkness of Abuse

Sim was born in Prince George, British Columbia, to traditional Sikh parents who were thrilled to have a girl join their rambunctious little boy. Shortly after this birth, there would be another son to make it a family of 3. They named their daughter Simarjeet, or Sim/Simi for short. The little girl grew up playing cops and robbers with her brothers, riding her banana-seat bicycle around the neighbourhood and running around like a little Tasmanian devil. She was a bundle of unbridled energy. She spoke loudly enough to be heard in rooms far removed from where she was, and one of her favourite pastimes was to jump off the roof of the shed onto her grandmother's garden. Interestingly, and unexpectedly, Sim was drawn to and excelled in playing the Indian drums, known as the tabla. It was altogether a fun, safe and secure childhood.

Life was golden until unexpected tragedy struck and her parents lost everything after the bankruptcy when Sim was in her teens. A wonderful childhood turned into teenage years of darkness and difficulty. Sim watched as her parents bravely struggled to stay afloat. The family couldn't afford their own house, so they were forced to rent and they jumped from basement to basement and home to home in search of affordable housing. At that time, Sim believed she was living through the darkest possible times. But when she became 19 years of age, her life took a different turn and darkness took on a more intense, more disturbing and life-threatening shade.

It wasn't apparent at first. Sim entered into an involved relationship, investing into the relationship a full eagerness to make it work, with the same gusto as she does everything else in life. What she ended up with instead was years of physical and emotional abuse.

In the early stages of the relationship, the two of them had money to burn. Their closets were filled with premium designer labels and the two of them together became hugely successful in business. She ran a fast-growing transportation company and had built a multi-million dollar portfolio in commercial and industrial real estate properties. And she was only in her early 20s. Yet all was not well on the domestic front. As time went by, the abuse ran deeper, the lies cut more deeply and, one day a few years into the relationship, Sim found herself on the wrong end of an aggressive and psychotic rage. In that moment, she decided that she had had enough and walked out with the clothes on her back, a sweater that was too thick for the British Columbia fall weather and sneakers on her feet. That's all she had and, by walking out of the door of her house, she turned her back on millions of dollars in business assets, all her belongings and irreplaceable life treasures.

To someone else, leaving so much in material possessions behind would have been deterrent. Sim thought differently — it was alright if she lost everything. She knew she could start over again with a clean slate. She was young, she was smart and she had guts to spare. Looking back, Sim believes that her true journey really began that day, when she reclaimed her inner strength to forge her own path, on her terms in life. Great business success would await her just a few years down the road. But on that day, all Sim knew was that she was her own woman again.

Timid Girl Finding Her Way in the World

Angie was raised in a non-traditional Chinese household and her parents were always supportive and fostered her interests, dreams and curiosities. Angie grew into a shy but joyful girl who always did her best, who strove for perfection in absolutely everything she was involved in, and always accepted a good challenge.

When she was 4 years old, her family realized that her immune system was severely vulnerable to a very common thing. Her peanut allergy was so severe that it was something that could endanger her life. She didn't have the same carefree approach to school lunches as did her peers. Because of her allergy, Angie became very observant of her surroundings and what was happening around her, and alert to details by the age of 5.

After graduating from high school, she launched herself into university and subsequently a French immersion program and began to really explore the world on her own. When she started her first job, Angie could tell that she didn't fit in with the nine-to-five crowd right away, but she wasn't sure how to move forward at that point. She felt stuck.

Looking for her calling, Angie dabbled in many things to broaden her horizon and to become well-rounded as an individual. She learned more about herself and about the real world when she got a job teaching and helping children with autism. Angie quickly learned that these children who were in some ways misunderstood were brilliant, perceptive, aware and sharp. They observed the world around them, and they knew what they were up against.

After Angie graduated university with a degree in Behavioural Neuroscience, she floundered a little. She had no interest in pursuing a master's in the field of Neuroscience as she wasn't passionate about research. She made two tries at a technical program, but had no luck there. Lost and searching, she took her mother's advice to become a mutual fund and life insurance agent. Angie did her research, got licensed and eased into the field. But though her big ideas to make her mark in the financial field didn't go as far as she hoped, she came away with some insights about herself:

First, Angie figured out what she loved, which is being in a position of authority where she can assist and educate others. When her friends came to her with investment questions and with queries about how to move forward with their finances, she was in her element. She gave good advice, and she helped her friends improve their financial situations.

Second, Angie realized, with much clarity, what she didn't want in her life. She was not cut out for any sort of life where she had to follow a template and walk other people's paths. She wanted to work for herself, and to work in a smart manner instead of trading long hours for wages.

Through trials, tribulations and more troubles than you can shake a stick at, Sim and Angie's lives crossed paths, and the rest would be history.

A Single Step Begins the Adventure

Your journey may be fraught with potholes and speed bumps but, once you get started with conviction and passion, no one can stop you. You are the only one who can control your destiny. We share below the words of the Chinese sage, Lao Tzu, in the hope that you will derive as much inspiration from them as we have:

Do the difficult things while they are easy and do the great things while they are small. A journey of a thousand miles must begin with a single step.

Where are you at in this moment in time? Are you living to survive or are you thriving in all aspects of life? Are you doing the work that you were told you were best suited for while knowing secretly in your heart that you could be so much more, or have you started carving your own path in life?

Look, we know that first step is hard, but you know what else is hard? Spending your entire life doing less than you can, and never really challenging yourself. What's hard is seeing chances go by and wondering "if only." What's hard is living in a world where you never get ahead.

When you think of it that way, taking that first step towards success sounds a lot less scary, doesn't it?

We started this journey years ago and, when we look back, the only thing we wonder is why we didn't do it sooner. Sure, it's scary, it's tough, and there are going to be nights where you just want to give up and cry yourself to sleep, but that's fine.

The only real thing to fear is a life of "not good enough" in your personal life and in your career or business. From where you are sitting, there is a whole world that is opening up for women just like you and, now that you've heard this call, you need to step up.

Don't be scared, be thrilled. Don't be uneasy, be bold. Your journey is just beginning. We invite you to take the first step with us.

* * *

Success Story from the Frontlines #1: Linda Ragsdale
Author, Illustrator, Founder of The Peace Dragon

Choices:
When the first round of machine gun fire stopped, an eerie silence paralyzed the restaurant.

In the moment of realizing my friends were all still alive – a new barrage began.

Shock. The gunfire was not moving away– it was coming towards us. The shooters were coming table by table to execute survivors.

So we waited.

This is not the beginning of a novel or a movie; this is a scene out of my life. If I lived, it would place me at a crucial point of power and choice– would the moment define me, or would I define the moment?

My sister and I had long ago discussed our journey through challenges. We realized each event in our lives should be greeted with a simple question, "What can we learn from this?" Each and every moment of our lives offers the ability to learn and move ahead, or anchor into an issue. We can either pack our luggage or collect the gems – trash or treasure time. Wouldn't you rather be holding a chest filled with pearls of wisdom than an overstuffed bag of unresolved issues?

It's funny because, at this time, I thought I had met all my life challenges – a violent ex-husband, miscarriages, family problems, business start-ups and closings, and a 14-year journey through the quagmire of diagnosing and alleviating an autoimmune disease. We all face similar trials, gratefully mixed in with the joyous bliss of our hopes which included for me: finding the right partner (and getting rid of the wrong one!); having children; and choosing a career that was play, never work. So far, I had been empowered by the bumps and blessings along the way. I was financially sound, and my dreams of being published, teaching, and dreams I hadn't dreamed had come true. Known for my perpetual smile, could I keep it after surviving a terrorist attack? Seeing all I had seen – could I find the treasure?

I had plenty of time to excavate. A single bullet seared a nearly three-foot path down my body. It ran one-quarter inch from my spinal chord, nicked my stomach, and exited out the top of my thigh. You need to excavate, sometimes through some heavy muck. Reflection is imperative because, if you don't travel through it, lessons will keep coming back wrapped in a new package. (How many of you have said, "Why does this keep happening to me?" or "How do these people keep finding me?") You must find your treasure! Even in the smallest fires of your life. When you do, all the mountains and fires that follow will seem small.

In my reflection, one crystal moment stands out from that night, my gem to share. After we escaped into the kitchen, the attackers came back with explosives. We escaped through a back hallway, where we exited through a door. One single doorway took us from the nightmare into the most beautiful night ever – chaos to calm. One doorway. So why would I ever go back through that door? What I took out of that room was my decision. I took love. I took hope. I took a mission to teach peace. After 4 years, I have spoken to and taught over 25,000 students and thousands of adults.

Choose joy. Choose happiness. Define your success by what you want, not others. Keep redefining it from the treasures you collect along the way, and share your gems.

And if you have some baggage, do yourself a favour – drop it off at the next doorway, open your treasure chest – and **smile!**

Chapter 2
Starve a Fear, Feed a Hope

When there's that moment of 'Wow, I'm not really sure I can do
this,' and you push through those moments,
that's when you have a breakthrough.

– Marissa Mayer

All the experiences you went through, the moments of failure
that you endured, and the choices you made have brought you
to where you are today. You don't often get what you think you
need in life; the universe serves you what it thinks you require
to become the best, most exciting, most expanded version of
yourself. In order to get to that point, you need to scale those
unexpected and infernal obstacles that crop up in your way. You
may do it clumsily and fall more times than you care to, or you
may do it with grace. Or, you may decide to stay put and let life
pass you by.

According to Forbes, the 3 scariest things in the world are
heights, spiders and snakes. Somewhere on the spectrum is
public speaking, and somewhere after that is death. However,
when you look closely at it, the biggest fears are the ones we

imagine, the ones that we conjure in our minds. Those are the ones that loom largest and most menacingly. You can side-step a spider or a snake and you can choose to stay on level ground. Those are easy enough decisions to make. But what about the fear of failure? The fear of success? The fear of being laughed at for wanting to be different?

Fear is Detrimental

What we're trying to get at here is that, when you stop and look at it, fear is something intangible that holds you back. In fact, that's putting it mildly. Fear puts you on a leash, it cages you and it makes you less than. When you are a female entrepreneur, you may find yourself stacked up against an unfriendly world. Fear tells you that you should be worried about being not strong enough, not smart enough, not experienced enough, not young enough, not beautiful enough and of course simply not competent enough. Does this mean that you should let these things stop you? Never!

As we talk to women, listening to their stories and learning why they are where they are, we have found that fear stops people in their tracks. Fear is this monster that they've made welcome in their homes, and they have fed it.

What we've both learned in our own experience, however, is that fear shouldn't be entertained, and it most definitely shouldn't pervade our lives. The problem with fear is that it takes up space in our minds and our hearts. A large fear is heavy and oppressive, and it squeezes out hope and ambition.

Neither of us have the time nor the space for fear, and neither should you. Let's talk about fear. Let's talk about what it is, what it does to us, and ultimately, how we toss it right out of our lives.

Both of us move forward focused on finding solutions. We don't live our lives looking over our shoulders for what could threaten us or what dangers lie around the corner that could trip us. If life throws us a soccer ball, we learn to kick it right back in a way that makes us feel powerful and invincible. Life without fear is liberating.

Naming the Beast: What is Fear?

When Angie was just a little girl, she developed an allergy that nearly killed her four times on separate occasions. A peanut allergy sounds harmless enough, but when you really think about how peanuts are everywhere, it becomes a nightmare. Most sweets were off the table and there were no ifs, ands or buts about it.

Angie's fear of peanuts was entirely legitimate. It was something that could endanger her life, and it was all around her, so what Angie's fear was doing was trying to keep her alive. It was trying to keep her away from something that she knew would hurt her.

At the most basic and primeval level, that is what fear does. It shows us something scary, and it says "Don't go near that thing because it could hurt you badly!" Our fears come from a very understandable and relatable place.

However, the thing to remember about fear is that it is not always right! Fear is not rational but, historically, it didn't need to be. Fear served an important purpose in our evolution, but now you need to see it for what it is.

Angie refused to live her life terrified of peanuts. Even as a little girl, she taught herself to read food ingredient labels diligently, and to be aware of her surroundings, especially when food was involved. She took steps to control her environment and to shrink her fear down to a pinpoint that was totally within her control.

The lesson she learned from her life-threatening allergy has gone on to help her face another fear in her life, which was stepping into a business venture she had absolutely no experience in.

Angie is considered by many to have an old soul, and getting involved with something completely out of her element where she had no certainty of the outcome was very unsettling and overwhelming for her. But knowing that she had in Sim a role model to look up to and a strong pillar to fall back on, she slowly pushed her boundaries further afield and absorbed as much knowledge and experience as she could. After many months and years of maturation in the field of business, Angie now knows with deep certainty there is nothing she cannot overcome, nothing she cannot conquer.

The Way Fear Changes Us

Remember how we talked about how fear's only purpose is to keep us alive? It doesn't care about how we are living as long as we are breathing, and frankly, as far as we're concerned, just breathing just isn't good enough!

It certainly wasn't good enough for Sim, when she was in her abusive relationship. Other women may have decided to stay in the abusive cycle where fear ruled their days, where the fear of something worse kept them living in perpetual misery. They may have been afraid of not being able to support themselves, or they stayed because of the children.

Sim decided to end the relationship, having finally realized that simply existing was just not enough. It is so easy for someone in Sim's shoes to play the victim card and lament that life was cruel. Instead, Sim took the fear she faced and turned it into motivation, into a positive force that compelled her to say "enough is enough." A fear of change could have kept her in a punitive relationship forever, but she planted her feet on the ground and decided that she would not live her life this way any longer.

During that time, Sim found herself gravitating towards higher education. At first she was drawn to psychology, to the disorders of the mind and how the mind worked. Then she found herself pulled towards criminology, where she could help women in her community facing domestic violence. Through it all, she was searching for herself. She learned a great deal in those classes but, more importantly, she learned that neither field was for her. She took the knowledge they offered and continued to forge a new path.

Fear in the Workplace

There are 2 very important types of fear in people at all times. We are afraid of rejection, and we are afraid of failure. Fear of rejection makes us afraid to act, and fear of failure makes us act hastily.

In many ways, being true to yourself means being willing to accept what is reality and what can't be changed, and to take action to change what can be altered in your life at that point in time. The world you create for yourself should suit you; if you are trying to make yourself suit your world, you are doing this out of fear.

What are you afraid of? If you are buckling under fear, there is a good chance that your way out is to simply keep everything as it is. That is how fear works, by controlling you and by making you jump through hoops to keep everything just right. Don't rock the boat, don't show too much of yourself, don't excel, don't do anything off the beaten track, don't be different.

If you stay on the conventional path, you think you'll be fine, but that is simply not true. You won't be. You'll just be on the same path as everyone else and you will never really uncover what you are truly capable of as an individual.

The Joy of Breaking Free

Now think about what happens if you see something glowing and wonderful off the beaten track. Maybe it's that business you've always wanted to start, maybe it's wanting to do better for the world we live in. Maybe it's wanting to live a life of adventure, to scale mountain peaks at altitudes where oxygen runs thin.

What it is that gets your heart racing, you can only accomplish by creating your own path. You need to break away from the crowd that you are running with and you may even have to tear yourself away from the people who are holding on to you. It's okay to go against the grain because it isn't until you are challenged that great things happen to you. Change doesn't occur until you take the initiative to liberate yourself from what is keeping you in place. All the power to make such changes is in your hands alone.

It's hard, and it's scary, but for the both of us, nothing has ever been more important.

Do you want to walk the same path for the rest of your life? We could comfort you by telling you that you could always go back to where you were before, but we know the truth.

Once you join us on the path less traveled, once you taste the freedom that shedding your fear gives you, you're never going to go back.

We sure haven't.

Getting Over Your Fear

If you haven't tapped into it, believe us when we say that will and power rest deep within you. You are capable of a force of self-will and inner power that you don't know about, and that strength and courage will kick in when you decide, like Sim did, that enough is enough. It's time to take charge of your own life and to live freely and fully.

Fear can have a physical grip on the body. All of us are at some time familiar with the so-called butterflies in the stomach, an accelerating pulse rate or the feeling as if the ground has opened under us. We now know feeling fearful triggers the release of stress hormones and other biochemical changes which brings the body into a state of hypervigilance.

For some of you, it is helpful to do breathing and relaxation exercises to calm the body and the mind. For others, affirmations or positive visualizations work. Sim certainly subscribes to taking pause to breathe deeply. If stress threatens to overwhelm, she escapes into her favourite place in nature, a detour which gives her the space and time to think, and to renew herself with positive energy.

The best way to overcome your fear is to take the first step towards your goal. Don't over-analyze the pros and cons. There will be critics telling you to stop, to go back or to rethink what you're wanting to do. Some of these naysayers may have a point, and you must pay some attention to what they say because they may offer a refreshing perspective that you've overlooked. But in the end, you must decide and you must make a move. Don't be so occupied in your thoughts that you never end up taking action.

Eleanor Roosevelt said it best when she said, "Do what you feel in your heart to be right – for you'll be criticized anyway. You'll be damned if you do, and damned if you don't."

One thing that holds so many great women back is that, even after they overcome the fear of change, fear's voice tells them to move slowly and cautiously.

We say why walk when you can run? Why run when you can fly? Women are defeated when they settle for dreaming small. Dream big. Make that leap because, once you have started, you might as well have it all!

Think of it like pulling off a bandage on a cut. Do you want to edge it off, millimetre by millimetre, or do you want tear it off all at once and get on with your day?

Your entire life is waiting, and the clock is always running. If you want to defeat your fear, you need to make that commitment to yourself and take action.

We're not saying this is easy, but we're saying it's worth it!

After Fear

Once you have taken that first step, you are going to look back and wonder what took you so long to get started. With that single step, no matter how small, you will see that you have grown, even if it was just a little bit. You are no longer the person who was imprisoned by fear and, once you take that step, you have it within you to stare fear in the face and tell it to shut up and leave.

After fear comes hope. Fear clouds your judgment under the guise of protecting you. Suddenly, all of the lies that fear was trying to tell you are rendered untrue. You will see that they were not protecting you; they were just keeping you in place, and this is where hope comes in.

For both of us, facing fear was what freed us. We each realized what was really holding us back and we took full ownership of the fact that we had allowed our fear to stymy our potential. When the fear fell from our eyes, we could see the world for what it really is – exciting, unexplored, brimming over with opportunities for us to grab. There was nothing standing in our way. There might have been a long journey ahead of us, but the way was clear. There were no monsters in our way, just challenges for us to meet head-on.

Right now, we ask you to put a face to your fear. Does it physically grip you and leave a knot in your stomach? Does it stop you in your mental tracks? Try this for a change. Think and feel deep down what you would feel if these symptoms of fear disappeared? What if the knot wasn't there? What if you were no longer afraid of what the neighbours would say? Isn't that liberating? If you were free and liberated, what would you be doing right now? What choices would you be making next? How would you be living? Remember, if you are living a life you are not satisfied with, maybe it's time to consider how fear may be affecting your life.

If you are afraid all of the time, your brain is constantly running and trying to manage those anxieties. When you let the fear go, you release both physical and mental stress. Fear is a choice. It is your choice and it is of your own making.

After we let go of that fear, everything opened up. There were tense times when we were getting our businesses started, and there were definitely a few nights when we wondered what we were going to do. Without fear, however, it simply became a challenge, one more thing for us to conquer and move on from.

Feeding Hope

Hope is a beautiful thing. It may be the size of the smallest seed when you take your first step on the journey, but that doesn't mean it's worthless. It only means that you need to nurture it and protect it. As with any other task, it is far easier to do it with 2 people than with one, and that is one of the many reasons why we are grateful we have found in each other a business partner to trust, to rely on and to build new worlds with.

Hope is something that you can nourish between yourself and a business partner that you trust completely. We've worked in dog-eat-dog environments where it was everyone for themselves, and the result was a place where everyone was focused on looking over their shoulders to see who would stab them in the backs. There was no trust, no team, and of course no hope.

If you have someone in your life you can trust, you can build hope. Be willing to reach out as we reached out to each other and as we are reaching out to you now. We believe that being an entrepreneur is a fine playing field for women who are looking beyond themselves and who are willing to work together to forge a brand new future.

When you let go of your fear, you will teach yourself to hope without bounds. When you shift your focus, great things start to happen.

Start with Hope to Get What You Want

Everything begins with hope.

If you have hope, you have the tool that will help you defeat fear. When you simply decide you are no longer fearful, the empty space that is left behind gets flooded with hope.

Have you given yourself permission to hope?

When was the last time you really hoped for something?

Are you afraid of hope, or are you afraid of your own power and ability to change your life?

Fear is Vexatious

Aren't you tired of fear yet? Are you drained by the way it controls you? We know that we were, so we decided to do something about it.

Neither of us has given fear a second thought in years. There are things that frustrate us, that bother us, and that make us frown, but nothing makes us afraid.

Let go of fear. We promise that you will love what your life becomes.

* * *

Success Story from the Frontlines #2: Shulei Chloe Tong President, Affinity Financial Services Inc.

I always had big goals and dreams. As I am a person who thrives on challenges, I felt the need to continue to better myself in my work and personal life. From 1992-1995, I resigned from 2 highly sought-after positions: one as a tax auditor with the Chinese Revenue Services in China, and the other as real estate project manager of a large corporation managing over $50 million worth of investment projects.

I left China for Singapore in 1995 to learn English while working in a futures exchange firm. I decided to explore Canada the year after as an International student because I wanted to experience life in the western culture. As a full-time student, I worked 2 jobs making $2500 a month to pay off my expensive tuition fees and living costs. I struggled financially but, even though my situation was bad, I always sent money back home so that my parents would have peace of mind thinking I was doing well in Canada.

Upon completion of my ESL program, receiving my BBA degree and being approved for Canadian residency, I immediately got on with pursuing my dream in the financial field. I was exhilarated and had a positive mindset moving onward, although my life was still fraught with challenges even after receiving my professional license in finances in 2001.

I began my business with 3 other partners and I felt like a superstar in my first year in the financial world, making over $100,000. But soon the stress and pressure was too much for all my partners to handle and they dropped out, leaving me with an 8000ft² office, a rental agreement to abide to, and other legal responsibilities to uphold. I had to take over all the loans and I maxed out all 10 of my credit cards to cover the monthly payments.

Despite the stress and hardship, nothing could have prepared me for the claw-back of over $100,000 in my 2nd and 3rd year as a life agent. There were countless nights where I felt so discouraged and cried myself to sleep. I gave myself a thousand reasons to give up and forget my dream. But it was never in my personality to quit. I loved what I did and continued to work hard at overcoming adversity.

I've lost a lot of money and shed many tears but, through the thick of it, I gradually progressed to earning a quarter of a million dollars in annual income a few years later. In 2009, I established my financial company, Affinity Financial Services Inc. The year after, I created my

Wealth Management Workshops. My success was growing faster than I could believe, and soon I found myself at the ranking of Top of the Table and became 1 of the top 10 recipients for the Outstanding Women of Canada award from the Chinese Women's Association of Vancouver. Every year since has been more successful than the last.

Looking back on the last 10+ years of my journey to wealth creation and success, I have failed countless times but I have also learned more than I ever could have if I had succeeded every step of the way. Money is only one aspect of business; what's more fulfilling is the power to impact my clients' lives for the better. To those who are starting their journey to achieving their biggest goals in life, I say: "Always have a dream, stay positive, stay focused, and never give up. Success will be yours."

Chapter 3
Jewels in the Dust

A woman is like a tea bag. You can't tell how strong she is until you put her in hot water.
– Eleanor Roosevelt

What image comes to mind when you come across the phrase, a wise woman? The typical description is that of an older woman who has achieved some measure of success, who has lived and loved and is surrounded by family and good friends. There is a great deal that we can learn from our elders, and both of us honour and respect the older women in our families, and where they have been.

Yet, to think that wisdom is only the province of our elders feels very limiting to us. Our female elders have cut a path through the world that inspires us and shown us how things were done once but, today, we are living in an entirely different world. It's wired, it's connected, and revolutions are started and ended through several taps on the keyboard. We have to cut our own paths and, in many ways, as we search for the wisdom to create our own businesses, we have to find our inspiration where we can.

The past is the past, but from it we can draw wisdom. There is wisdom all around us if we know how to look for it. We've found wisdom with our mentors, with our elders, with people barely half our age, and in the very world around us.

In this chapter, we talk about wisdom and the lessons we can learn in the strangest places.

Children So Often Misunderstood

When Angie spent time working with children with autism, she knew she was going to be the teacher. She was working with children who needed help with basic tasks. Some of them might never be able to live without assistance, and many of them would face challenges with interpersonal relationships as they grew up.

Angie was ready to help them tackle the world but, to her surprise, it was the kids who taught her a valuable lesson. Working with them reshaped her perspective about her future, and she changed course from one that she was drifting into, to one that stirred the depths of her heart and soul.

What she learned was that, because of the way they were perceived, people constantly underestimated these kids. The world saw them as being radically different because society could not understand what the kids were saying or doing.

As a matter of fact, the opposite was true. Though these children had some level of difficulty with communication, and though they expressed themselves in ways that were deemed problematic or unacceptable, they were sharply perceptive and finely aware of the world around them. They observed and spotted details and minutiae that other people would miss. Their minds worked in unique ways, and this assisted them in processing data in a very focused way.

As Angie worked with these children, she realized that, sometimes, teachers come into our life in the most unexpected of places, and that wisdom can be delivered by the youngest and most innocent among us. Wisdom is not only the privilege of a hermit or guru who has renounced the world for caves in high places. Sometimes, the simplest and most potent pieces of wisdom are offered to you from someone who is very different from you. What you receive then are different ways to view the pieces of a puzzle.

Finding Wisdom in Unexpected Places

Corporate wisdom tells us to think outside of the box, but most people don't go far enough. You will find wisdom from the strangest sources and opportunities. For instance, Candice Carpenter, who co-founded iVillage, found her inspiration while she was climbing mountains.

"My character was formed by mountaineering. Enduring rainy slopes and cold bivouacs to spend an hour at the top of the world shaped my ability to handle adversity," Carpenter states with pride.

Dealing with heavy packs and cold icy weather has nothing to do with founding a successful company, but Carpenter's story says differently. Her history in the mountains taught her to be strong, just like Angie's experience taught her to be patient, aware, and sensitive to people's body language.

Think about the experiences you have had, and remember that lessons come for you at the strangest times. There is no such thing as a wasted experience if you see with the right eyes and an open heart.

Creating Your Own Wisdom

As a woman entrepreneur, you must be willing and able to find your lessons when they come to you. Because there are so few women entrepreneurs comparatively at this point, you must be willing to be something of a pioneer.

Figures from Industry Canada showed, at the end of 2011, women-owned small businesses stood at only 17% of all small business firms. We are still small in numbers. There are not volumes and volumes of books offering us wisdom. Instead, we must find it on our own.

If Angie had seen those children as incapable of teaching her anything, she would never be as observant and as aware a woman as she is today. The lessons they taught her will stay with her forever.

Was there a time when you were surprised by someone's wisdom offered through a different point of view? Did you take the lesson as it was offered, or did you turn away from it because this person was cast from a different mold? When you stray off the path, you must be willing to accept wisdom from strange and unexpected sources and places. Teachings may be sourced from people who are very different from you. They offer you different pieces of a puzzle and different ways of being fulfilled or successful.

Under African Skies

In December 2009, Sim decided to stretch her boundaries far and wide into new territory. The farthest from Canada she had travelled was India. However, the timing was not right. So she placed the dream under her pillow and moved on with the rest of her life.

A place where life is lived close to the bone, where basic resources like water and food are in short supply, may seem like an odd place for a young entrepreneur. But that was where Sim learned her biggest lessons. In 2011, she went to West Africa to mentor young women. Having had her own run-in with financial difficulties, Sim thought she understood what not having enough might feel or look like. In Ghana, her worldview changed when she lived with a family who had next to nothing.

When Sim first arrived in Accra, Ghana's capital, she had no concept of what was in store for her. The water was cold, the food, for the most part, simple and bland, she had to take cold showers, and the people and culture were vastly different from cosmopolitan Vancouver. Her host family lived off a daily income of a few dollars a day. They didn't have a car, and the home had the barest basics. Sim's room had bare concrete walls and the only piece of furniture was a simple bed made of a single piece of plywood placed on a brittle wood frame. She had only a thin blanket to fend off the cold at night.

Yet, Sim saw that they were a happy bunch. Rather than constantly bemoaning what they lacked, the people she lived with knew and treasured what was truly precious in their lives. They lived so close to the edge of poverty, something that Sim had never experienced before, even if her family was roughing it out in her teens. At the same time, the lack of material possessions was inconsequential. She saw a strength in her host family that was rooted in focusing on what was important and meaningful to them, which was family, community, a connection to nature and to each other. Consequently, there was little fighting about silly, unimportant issues, and none or little of the meaningless arguments that would befall a poor family in Canada.

Her host family really made a positive impact on her. Observing at close quarters how they derived much joy from the simplest pleasures in life, Sim left Ghana with a deep appreciation that life was always rich, no matter how big or small the bank account was. At the same time, that realization drove her to make the best of her own life and the opportunities that would come before her. It spurred her to create a future where she would be her own boss, rather than be an employee, and where she could create wealth and plenty for herself and her family. She also saw success as an instrument through which she could do more good in her community.

Knowing What You Truly Want

Sim flew back to Canada with a fire in her heart. Before she left, she had started another trucking company with her father and brother. During the time she was in Africa, the company operated with only 3 trucks. On her return, she steered the business to a whole new level. Now the business is worth millions with increasing revenues year after year.

Africa was an awakening experience. She realized more keenly that she was capable of so much more, and she was lucky enough to live in a country where opportunities and possibilities abound. It was just up to her to grab them. Of course, there were moments when doubts crept in and she questioned herself. During those moments, Sim trusted her energy and her inner guidance, and the direction it was taking her naturally.

As women entrepreneurs, we are focused on plenty and on acquiring wealth, power and respect in our fields.

This is the goal, but it is important to remember what that goal stands for. You want more money and more respect, but why do you want them?

For Sim, her failed relationship, her financial problems and her African trip added threads to the warp and weft of the tapestry that was becoming her life. She never saw her problems as failures on her part; instead she viewed them as blessings through which she came into her own as a woman with her own voice and a determination to make the best of the life and gifts she had been given.

Many women entrepreneurs chase random goals down the wrong path. They think that taking this job will make them respected or that doing this training will prepare them for a prestigious position. They don't think about why they want these things, or how it will help their lives later on.

Everything we do, we do for a reason. If you are an entrepreneur, you cannot waste motion, time or effort chasing random goals down the wrong path. Reflect inside why you are starting your business. Is it because that is the conventionally acceptable thing to do or is it because the business fires you with passion?

The Law of Cause and Effect

Here is something to ponder: The Law of Cause and Effect tells us that often the troubles that ail are of our own making. As such, no one, absolutely no one, can fix your problems, except yourself.

When the two of us came across that piece of wisdom, things fell into place. Life can be tough and, sometimes, we were guilty of making it harder on ourselves. When we accepted responsibility for the things that happened, we were able to make the big changes that would turn things around. This piece of wisdom came to us at just the right time, and now we are passing it on to you.

What are you holding on to? How have you caused your own problems? How can you let go?

Learning From Everything

Some way, somehow, you found your way to us. Maybe you liked the cover of this book, or maybe our book was recommended to you by a friend. We're here to guide you to uncover your dreams and passions and to live a more productive and successful life, but we're not your final authority.

What you need are people in your life who will lead you by example and help you find your own way towards something amazing. This is why you need to recognize your teachers and to really identify the wisdom that comes your way.

Opportunities Surround You

Life is full of opportunities; we both believe that very much. When we met, we knew at once that we had found something special. Angie admired Sim's spirit and courage, and Sim was drawn in by Angie's determination and patient resolve. Angie provided the ground that Sim needed to soar, and Sim gave Angie the push towards adventure that Angie had always wanted.

We found wisdom and power in each other. For us, our partnership is something that instructs us and guides us every day.

Look all around you for the wisdom that the universe is sending you. Both of us very firmly believe that things happen for a reason, and whatever you choose to call this force, it is one that exerts a very real pull on you.

Deciding to walk our talk, one day we decided to call on this force...in our own way. While walking through a park, we decided to have a chat with the universe, with no holds barred. We climbed onto a large rock, held hands to align our energies, looked up at the sky and started a very vocal and verbal conversation with the universe. It didn't matter if passers-by thought we were soft in the head; what mattered was that we wanted to speak to the universe that way, and we did. We often have a good laugh about it but what matters most to us is that we did what we were stirred to do. As crazy as it may have been, it felt good speaking loudly and directly to the universe.

Wisdom in Unexpected Quarters

Not many of us would consider Youtube a library of wisdom, but that's how it happened for Angie. Unable to sleep, Angie was checking out Youtube videos when she came across a Brian

Tracy video about the secrets of self-made millionaires. Intrigued, inspired and motivated by the rags-to-riches stories of millionaires who achieved success on their own terms, Angie stayed up to watch the 46-minute video in full. She learned so much in three-quarters of an hour than she had in the years of education. When she woke up the next day, she felt charged and excited about the potential that lay within her. She had previously given self-development a miss, but her world changed in less than an hour.

Angie didn't waste any time implementing what she learned that night. She made a choice to see the good in everything and in everyone, and to pursue her life with zest and passion. Her effervescence rubbed off on Sim and life became easier, more fun, and more adventurous.

Right now, think about a memory, anything that stays with you for some reason. Perhaps it was something that a parent or caregiver said to you a long time ago. Perhaps it was simply noticing the way that the light was coming through the trees. Perhaps it was a single conversation you had with someone not all that long ago.

The understanding, knowledge and experiences that stick with us do so for a reason. If there is a recurrent pattern in the signals, it is the universe trying to reach us, to make us aware of what we may need to help us tackle and surpass challenges on our journey in life. When you express the wish to be successful to the universe, the universe sends back tips and hints on how you can accomplish it.

What you need to do is to sharpen your awareness—take your horse-blinders off—and heighten your listening skills. Open yourself up to what the world is trying to tell you, and do not spare too much angst about the packaging.

Finding Gems

You are ready to listen, but maybe you are unaware of how to do it. Are you worried that messages and signs are passing you by? This is something that we encounter a lot, and it is very common among women who are ambitious. There is nothing as terrifying or as frustrating, after all, as a missed opportunity!

Here's the secret. When the message comes and you hear it, that is exactly what it was meant to be. Just be open and receptive. When you do this, you will catch exactly what you are meant to catch.

For example, when you walk out your door today, be open to what happens. Pay attention to the world, and think about the people who talk with you and who want to interact with you. How do they affect you and how do they make you feel?

When something troubles you, make a note of it. When something pleases you and makes you laugh, pay attention to it. Be especially cognizant during times of failure, and consciously understand the core reasons why something happened the way it did. Remember, failures aren't meant to be received as punishment, but rather learning moments that better prepare us for future challenges. As you move forward towards your destiny, you will find that it is life's small moments, piled up one after another, that make us who we are. The gems of wisdom that we gather are what make us unique.

There is something to be taken from every interaction. There is a lesson to be learned in the things we notice and the way we move forward. Think hard about your life right now. If you feel like you are 'stuck,' lost and searching, or ready to better yourself, that means you are ripe for the message the universe is sending to you. We've both found an amazing value in being open to the wisdom of the universe. Sometimes all it takes is meeting the right person. Sometimes all it takes is hearing the right piece of music or spotting the right thing.

An Interesting Woman Lives Life on Her Terms

Women need to stop caring about what others think and live for themselves. More importantly, you have to accept that you are not perfect; you never will be. Sim was always focused on perfection and never wanted to look like a failure. So, for a time, she put up with an empty, loveless and abusive relationship. She became depressed and felt empty of any emotions. Well, she had a wakeup call and a nasty one at that, when she found herself physically threatened.

When she moved on from her abusive past and looked towards her future, Sim's life became far more interesting and meaningful as a result.

Let us say this, an interesting woman is far more attractive and compelling than a perfect one.

There is wisdom all around you, so start accessing it. Be an active listener when the world speaks and, soon enough, your path forward will be as clear as daylight.

Chapter 4
Making an Ally of Time

Your journey has molded you for your greater good, and it was
exactly what it needed to be. Don't think you've lost time. There is
no short-cutting to life. It took each and every situation you have
encountered to bring you to the now. And now is right on time.

– Asha Tyson

Time is a gift, and we have learned that there is no such thing as
wrong timing. Without time, there could be no forward
motion—you would always be at a standstill, locked into one
moment and one experience.

With the dimension of time, however, your life gains texture and
depth, giving you a fuller range of experiences. There are times
when you laugh, times when you cry, times when you dust
yourself off after failure, and times when you celebrate.

Your relationship with time is your choice; it is always up to you
how to spend your time. We have learned that we are the ones
who decide when to seize an opportunity, when to push
through, and when to get what we want. For women as well as

everyone else, there is only now, so when will you decide that your moment has come?

Your Right Time Has Come!

In January 2014, Forbes Magazine launched a bright and celebratory article about women entrepreneurs. In "11 Reasons 2014 Will Be A Breakout Year For Women Entrepreneurs,"[1], it pointed to the explosive 57% increase in women-owned firms valued at $10 million or more. True, these numbers pertain to women business owners in the U.S., where conditions are favourable to female entrepreneurs. Still, in this interconnected age, women around the world can draw inspiration from their American sisters.

Women business owners are part of a growing wave, and their numbers continue to increase steadily. Statistics Canada figures show that, in 2012, there were 950,000 self-employed women, representing 36% of all self-employed entrepreneurs.[2] Women own 47% of all small- to medium-sized businesses (SMEs), and SMEs that are either majority or fully owned by women contribute $117 billion to Canada's economic output every year.

[1] http://www.forbes.com/sites/geristengel/2014/01/08/11-reasons-2014-will-be-a-break-out-year-for-women-entrepreneurs/ accessed August 29 2014
[2] http://www.owit-ottawa.ca/wp-content/uploads/2014/03/Facts-and-figures-on-women-entrepreneurs.pdf

These are by no means small figures, but we in Canada can still draw inspiration from equally remarkable trends that are taking place globally.

Around the world, women are proving to be extremely effective at generating profits and returns on capital invested in their companies. We are seeing a wave begin to crest as women entrepreneurs around the world are stepping up to the plate. They are shattering what remains of the glass ceiling as they pave the way for limitless growth of new businesses large and small.

The winds of change are also whistling through the cracks in the glass ceiling with the end result that top business leaders are embracing more feminine values such as cooperation, consensus, trust, global vision and reciprocity. In the book *Spend Shift: How the Post-Crisis Values Revolution Is Changing the Way We Buy, Sell, and Live*, authors John Gerzema and Michael D'Antoni argue that such feminine values have fueled the post-global crisis recovery. With findings based on a survey of 64,000 people in 13 countries, the authors saw that, as consumers adapted to the crisis by seeking more balance and fulfillment in their lives, they were more willing to support those companies that advocated transparency, ethics and sustainability. At the same time, two-thirds of the respondents in the survey said that the values they wanted in corporate leaders included patience, intuition, flexibility and empathy, traits normally considered as feminine. In order to reconnect with these consumers, who are voting with their dollars every day, companies are intentionally prioritizing values over profits.

In other words, feminine values are on the rise in the corporate culture. Old, masculine notions of competition, secrecy and control are giving way to values, connection, relationship-building and community.

When is it Right Timing?

Some people pin their success on being in the right place at the right time. But success should never be dependent only on luck. Yes, there is certainly an element of luck, but we must put in the blood, sweat and tears to stack the dice in our favour before we roll them and hope for the best. This way, when luck does strike, you are ready to seize the opportunity and run with it.

Don't hold yourself back waiting for that right moment to strike. Many successful people have made it by hitting the ground running, even if the timing was imperfect. They may not have had all the right answers all of the time, but they made sure to maintain forward motion no matter what. It's only when you make a choice to take action that your next steps can become clear.

To succeed, you need to connect the dots. You need a panoramic view that takes in past, present and future. When your energy is flagging and you want to give up, take a moment to look back and acknowledge how much you have gained and grown since you first started. In order to stay the course, you need to appreciate the past, then look into the future to be reminded of your vision. The most effective actions are taken from a place of presence, with a perspective on the past and future in mind.

There will be times when you will need to forge ahead alone, because only you can see the vision into which your business will grow. There will be times when you have to look to outside talent in order to expand a fast growing company with grace and efficiency. There may be times when you bounce back from crushing failure, and there will be times when you need to mature, to develop more nuances to your game. When you appreciate these opportunities as the gifts they are, you will succeed in making time your ally.

Right Timing Also Means on the Right Day

Where other women learn by jumping in headlong and making mistakes, Angie takes a more considered and thoughtful approach. For her, the old soul that she is, every experience contains a learning that will benefit her, if not immediately, then further down the road. She has a special ability to connect cause and effect, and to learn by observing others, both of which work in her favour. She takes the best from the models she admires and respects, and sidesteps mistakes by avoiding the errors made by others. Observation pays off for Angie.

Guided by her inner truth and knowing, Angie made her way carefully through various fields of work over a period of several years. In the financial and insurance sectors, she felt she had finally found professional true love. But after a year, the infatuation began to wear off, and the desire to shake things up emerged once again.

In this day and age when we feel so much pressure to 'have it all figured out,' it takes great strength to live with not knowing. Yet Angie never forgot to look inward for direction, trusting that she would be shown what she needed to know, when she needed to know it. Others might have become frustrated with their lot and given into convention by settling for a profession that was comfortable and provided decent pay. However, Angie saw her professional detours as valuable preparation for something better, and never failed to learn all she could from each experience. She knew from the moment that she stepped out of her comfort zone, she was getting closer and closer to discovering her true purpose and calling in life.

When Angie met Sim, she had sufficient financial savvy to fully appreciate Sim's creativity in devising smart and original real estate investing strategies to create win-win situations for everyone involved.

As Angie muses, "I observed how she implemented certain strategies and helped families solve their real estate issues, and I was very intrigued. Sim taught me while she learned, keeping me in the loop. How great it was that she wanted me to learn with her along the way, for neither of us foresaw that we would be working really closely with each other in real estate the following year."

A seed had been sown. What appeared to be a commonplace business meeting turned out to be the beginning of a powerful business partnership. Angie had recognized a kindred spirit, and knew that the time was right to step into new possibilities by embarking on a real estate venture with Sim. In this way, she took advantage of the opportunities the moment presented to move things in a new direction.

Was there a time in your life when you waited for the "right" moment? When that moment came, did you seize it?

Timing is Everything

When Sim's realtionship ended, she didn't see it as the end of all that was good in life. Instead, she chose to embrace it as the beginning of a new, bolder and better passage of life. When she couldn't get into policing despite months of preparation, Sim decided that it was time to fulfill a desire, which was to go to Africa to mentor and empower young women and to help them build self-esteem and confidence.

She was in no great rush to reforge her own business after the breakup. Always in ownership of her own life, she strongly felt instead that the time was right to help young women in the way she had always dreamed of. As she puts it, "I had decided that I would never look back, but instead move forward to better my life!"

As far as she and the young women she helped were concerned, she arrived neither too early nor too late, but right on time. Sim recognized that the time had come to live her life on her own terms, to be her own boss, and to make her own decisions. It took her two years after her breakup to arrive at the point where it was time to reconstruct her businesses.

Without making this string of decisions, she would never have met her business partner, Angie. Her teaming up with Angie coincided with her decision to diversify her investments with real estate. Transportation was in Sim's blood; her father had started a transportation company when she was just a few months old, and toy cars and trucks, not dolls, were her favourite toys. Although she took to property investing like a duck to water, Sim recognized that a partnership would be advantageous. She was ready to expand and, when she found a partner she could trust, she didn't hesitate.

So, are you ready to take ownership of your success? If not now, then when?

Understanding Time

In the West, people believe that time is linear, a continuous line travelling out of the past and into the future. In the East, however, people view time as circular, believing that patterns naturally repeat at a personal and collective level; what has come before will come again. It might be more accurate to say that, in the East, we view time as a spiral, knowing that we may repeat certain encounters or challenges over and over again, but the precise forms these experiences take will evolve. We recognize that our perspective naturally expands with time, and that later experiences will have a different flavour from our earlier ones just because we are that much more experienced, skillful, and courageous.

Both of us are the products of what our lives have been. Everyday, we acquire experiences and feelings, goals and ambitions that make us subtly different from who we were the previous day. It's not that we're changeable or fickle; rather, we are simply human, and every experience, outcome, and choice adds more texture to who we are. Every second in our lives enriches us to become better and more powerful as co-creators. We learn to trust and believe in ourselves with every moment fully lived.

If we had tried 10 years ago to do what we are doing now, our interaction would most likely have been less productive. Now, Angie brings her perseverance and her keen observation skills to the table, assets that took time to hone. Sim brings her guts and grit, qualities that have been enhanced and strengthened through the paths she took in life.

The Blame Game is a Waste of Time

It is easy to look back and play the blame game. If only I hadn't wasted so much time! If only I had done something earlier! If only I had listened to my intuition. If only, if only – these words of regret are words of waste. They do nothing to advance you towards your goals, and they demolish your self-esteem. Regret keeps you living in the past, when it's the present moment and possibilities it holds for the future that are worth living for.

We don't believe that time is ever wasted. When you don't do something, there is a very good chance that you are just not ready to do it. It means that, right now, at this juncture in your life, you are still sowing the ground. It's not that you are not doing anything; you are instead carefully cultivating the seed of possibility, and feeding it. You are still tending to your garden and you are waiting for the right time to harvest. As any good farmer or gardener knows, there is no rushing this process—the key is to cultivate under ideal conditions to support the seeds you plant in order for them to express their true nature.

Taking Ownership of Each Moment in Time

Note there is a difference between foolishly jumping in with both feet, and taking a considered risk. We are all for well-researched and calculated risks. Risks are part of living large, but it is the way you assess risk that can make the difference. When you live in regret of the past, your life is governed by fear of repeating past mistakes, which defeats the purpose of learning from them. When you decide that risk is to be avoided, that decision takes you away from the expanded life you secretly long for. But when you live in the present, your view of the world changes. You may then perceive that the risk before you is far more manageable than it may appear on first assessment.

How does that come about?

When you are in the moment, you are not torn by regret, but you bring the expanded awareness you gained from past choices to the decision before you.

When you live in the moment, you create a magical space for yourself in which you are fully in touch with who you are, the gifts that life has given you, and the wisdom and experience you have earned. Risk looks different from this space, because you have taken ownership of the moment.

Now is Your Time

These words ring with great truth for us: "Everything, in the end, comes down to timing. One second, one minute, one hour could make all the difference."

We say to you that everything in your life has been leading you to this point. It may be a point where you are leaving comfort and convenience behind to live the life of the nomad, to see the world. It may be a point where you decide to go back to school, even though most of your classmates will be half your age. Little is to be gained by dwelling in the past to see what you could have done differently. There is no going back to where you were, and no amount of wishing will ever change this. There is only learning from past mistakes and moving forward into the future. Perhaps you are afraid you will fail, or perhaps you are simply unsure of what success will look like.

We say to you this: Trust that, at this moment, you have all the tools you need to take the next step that is waiting for you. Angie's keen eye and Sim's courageous optimism are the legacies they took from their old lives and used as tools to carve out the path that has led them to where they are today.

Step Up to the Plate in the Right Way

You have come forward to this place and time with a purpose, and now the time has come to seize it. It is time for you to take your place among the growing ranks of women entrepreneurs.

We don't believe in pressure. If you're not ready, you're not ready. It doesn't mean that you'll never be ready, and of course it doesn't mean that you are a failure. We strongly believe that only you can define what success means to you.

However much time has gone by, remember that there is no such thing as too late. If you are reading and feeling the resonance of our words, you understand that the greatest gift you can give to yourself is to consciously choose what to make of the moment life presents you with now.

What you need to do is to tell yourself how perfect it is, and how you are in the perfect place for what you want to do and who you want to be. You are the sum total of your experiences so far, containing infinite potential that can be birthed only by you.

At this moment, you are standing on the cusp of something great. Sim and Angie recognized their moment and, when they seized it without hesitation, they created a partnership that would send out positive ripples throughout their community and the world.

Letting Go of Control is the Right Way

You can't control timing. You can't control when the chance of a lifetime strikes. You can never get back the time you've lost. You can, however, control how you choose to respond to the opportunity that awaits you precisely at this point in time.

Life is complicated but, in the end, the pieces fall into place and fit together like laser-cut puzzle pieces, if you give them the space and the time to do so.

It begins with trust.

Trust that you are meant to be here in this moment right now, and trust your next steps, as long as they are made in alignment with your deep beliefs in who you are and who you want to be. Trust like Sim did when she found that she wasn't meant to go into policing, and chose instead to become an entrepreneur. Trust like Angie did when she left the financial field for another path that stirred her passion.

Let go of the idea that you should have done this, or that you should not do that. Instead, embrace and love who you are, right now.

The time is right. The time is now. It's your time to move forward with purpose.

* * *

Success Story From The FrontLines #3: Laurie Finnigan
Director of Operations, Legacy Wealth Income Properties

As I get older, I strive towards living in the now and creating a more purposeful life. I have always felt that I am here to make an impact in a larger way, and I take great joy in helping people get unstuck and better their lives. A big turning point in my life was when I received a call from my mother (while I was spending my 8th year working abroad in the Caribbean) informing me that my father had a severe stroke just shortly after he retired at the age of 68. The stroke affected both my parents' quality of life in a drastic way, and so I decided it was time to move back home. I wanted to continue living an adventurous and exciting life, and I knew I did not want to be stuck in the rat race, so I strived for financial independence. My father's stroke has been the biggest catalyst to encourage and drive me to live in the now and design the best life possible, and inspire others to do the same.

I was always intrigued by the stock market, and I found myself with a career in the financial industry, which for the most part I felt was a man's industry at that time, and predominantly still is today. I was always the assistant to the professional, which in most cases were men, and I felt I was never treated equally. There were times when I passed up on opportunities because I feared I was not capable of succeeding, and I worried how others would think of me if I failed. Looking back now, I realize I did not have a strong team of like minded people and mentors in my life to boost me up when I was feeling deflated and insecure. My close friends and family did not really understand me because I think an entrepreneur's mind is so very different from the norm, which didn't make things any easier.

I was living in Antigua in 2008 when the financial crisis happened. So many lives were affected and destroyed; even till this day many people have not recovered, and some never will. I watched my own RRSPs drop in value by 90%, and the luxury residential development I was managing came to a complete halt. I had to start all over from scratch and reinvent myself. I often refer to the saying, "no evolution without shock:" Most people wait until something really drastic happens before they wake up and make a change. My drive and passion in life propelled me through the struggles I faced, and I eventually took ownership of my dream and goals to help people live better lives through real estate, by starting my own real estate investing business.

I do my best to overcome adversity by not dwelling on things for too long, and I know that I just have to push forward no matter the struggles. We will always be faced with challenges throughout our lives so we have to learn to pick up and move on and understand that it is all part of the journey in life and success. Surround yourself by love, take good care of your health, and make sure to associate yourself with friends and business partners who align with your values, interests, and goals. To live life to the fullest, we have to take risks, evolve, expand, and seize opportunities that take us out of our comfort zone.

Chapter 5
Going with the Beat

Women observe subconsciously a thousand little details, without knowing they are doing so. Their subconscious mind adds these little things together – and they call the result intuition.

– Agatha Christie

A spider's web is a miracle at work. If you've ever seen one illuminated in the morning light, you likely noticed that each strand is anchored and woven to support another. Viewed through human eyes, the delicately crafted web is a work of art. From a fly's perspective, however, the spider's web is a deadly trap.

No one taught the spider how to weave. It emerged from an egg already knowing how to produce silk, and how to use that beautiful but deadly resource to create a home and a trap for its food. It has the built-in ability to unreel this silk on demand, whose tiny tendrils are built to absorb impact without breaking the integrity of the web's structure.

By obeying its instincts and following the inner guidance that only it can hear, the spider creates a work of art every day. As humans we don't have the instincts to create this kind of miraculous web, but it IS within our instincts to unleash our potential and excel beyond our wildest dreams!

Intuition Lights the Way Forward

Brain studies suggest that men's and women's brains are wired in different ways. Increasingly sophisticated technology such as positron-emission tomography (PET) and functional magnetic resonance imaging (fMRI) are producing findings that show astonishing variations in the brains of males and females.

A study of the brains of 1000 adolescents published in the magazine *Scientific American*[3] revealed that female brains exhibit more connections between the left and right hemispheres, and scientists believe this optimizes the ability of women to combine analytical and intuitive thinking. Imaging experiments by Dr. Jill Goldstein of Harvard Medical School show that male and female brains have quite different architecture. Women's brains are bulkier in the frontal and limbic cortices.[4] These are the brain

[3] http://www.scientificamerican.com/article/how-mens-brains-are-wired-differently-than-women/, accessed August 30, 2014
[4] http://www.scientificamerican.com/article/his-brain-her-brain-2012-10-23/?page=2, accessed November 30, 2014

centres that deal with higher cognitive functions such as language, judgment, planning and control, and emotional responses, thus explaining why women are stronger in intuition, collaboration and empathy.

A woman's instincts are among her most powerful tools. Women are known for placing more value on their intuition; however, in the rough and tumble world of business, women's instincts are too often dismissed as flights of fancy, with greater credence paid to facts and numbers. Women who said "they feel" were previously shut down by bosses who wanted proof, rather than feeling. Nonetheless, we feel we are in the midst of a change. As we pointed out in Chapter 4, feminine values are increasingly being embraced in a changing workplace. Additionally, intuition has been given the thumbs-up by revolutionary business icons such as Steve Jobs, who said, "I began to realize that an intuitive understanding and consciousness was more significant than abstract thinking and intellectual logical analysis. Intuition is a very powerful thing, more powerful than intellect, in my opinion. That's had a big impact on my work."

This is what we believe: No matter what you call them, your instincts can serve you very well as you set off down your entrepreneurial path. Statistics and numbers describe situations that have already happened. The call to greatness takes you into the future, but you don't have to go into it blind-folded. The little voice in your head that cheers you on or warns you of danger can and should be the sharpest tool in your box.

We believe that successful people are always busy. They are always thinking, moving and working towards the future they see, while average people do the bare minimum and complain about it. We have been compelled to always look towards the future, which is where our vision lives, so we can act today to bring it to fruition.

Your Intuition Directs You to True North

Often described as a small, quiet voice, your intuition is your best compass when you are unsure which direction to go in. Each of us experiences it differently.

It may be a gentle voice. It may be a tugging at the guts. It may be a sudden flash, a revolutionary thought that takes you out of your boxed thinking, and before you know it, you've found the solution to a perplexing problem.

We would like to direct you to the words of one of the world's greatest minds, Albert Einstein, who said, "No problem can be solved from the same level of consciousness that created it." For us, this means that you have to think outside of the confined structures that created the problem in the first place. Your intuition comes as a great and reliable tool to use when logic alone does not suffice.

Uncaging the Lioness

Sim has always been in tune with her instincts. However, through being served unexpected blows and several knocks, she found her intuition being sharpened and refined and, in time, she came to trust her inner voice, absolutely and wholeheartedly.

Sim followed her instincts and abandoned an unhealthy relationship before things got out of hand. It didn't matter if she had absolutely no idea about her next steps. All she knew was that, when she took back control of her life, she felt like a lioness uncaged from a prison, finally able to live and roam freely in the jungle, her natural habitat. So she pushed through her misgivings.

She tamped down any distracting voices and followed her instincts as they guided her out the door, leaving the past solidly where it belonged...in the past. She took relevant lessons with her into a future that held new opportunities and true happiness.

No longer a little mouse who feared a cat lurking around every corner, she came to view herself as a lioness with skills and power equal to just about anyone. There was nothing she couldn't do when she owned her own power.

Her instincts led her first to the police force, and then on to Africa. The woman she had been before would have endlessly questioned her capabilities and the wisdom of getting into such new and untried territory. But the woman she had become, the one who listened and trusted her inner urges, looked at all those challenges, smiled, and thought, "I can handle all of this!"

On her return to Canada from Africa, Sim found herself once again attracted to transportation and real estate. Instead of fighting this instinct or overanalyzing the risks and rewards, she jumped in with both feet, and that's how Sim and Angie's business ventures began.

Like a Light Shining Out

Angie has always been a little reserved, a little withdrawn and careful about what she does. In many ways, this is her strength, as she looks before she leaps, and she always knows what's going on around her. However, it wasn't until she was a university student studying Behavioural Neuroscience that she had her first brush with her own powerful instincts.

Angie loves academia. She believes strongly that education will elevate us in ways that we never dreamed, and that knowledge is one of the most enduring types of power there is.

However, one day, as she was walking across campus, she was struck by an epiphany. She loved writing reports and learning about the brain, but she simply did not want to spend the next few years of her life in school. She foresaw that further studies in university would require an enormous expenditure of time, money and energy that would yield little returns. This path she was on was not going to launch her into a job she would be remotely interested in. She preferred to work smarter by putting her intellect to work finding the right career.

This was a groundbreaking realization for Angie. Suddenly, she knew that she didn't want to continue on to a master's degree, and she didn't want the life that came after it.

Some people would have continued on anyway, dismissing this revelation as a baffling and disruptive quirk that needed to be ignored. They would have buried this impulsive thought under a mountain of logic and rationale and never looked at it again.

Angie, however, did not do any of this. She didn't run from her own impulses, but she didn't ignore them either. Instead, she sat down and carefully thought out a plan. She decided she would finish her undergraduate degree while working as a neurology research coordinator at the University of British Columbia Hospital, while she kept an eye out for other options.

There are many ways to react to your instincts, and Angie chose the route that she knew would work for her. She figured out what she did not want, and when she was crystal-clear about that, she switched her focus to what she did want. She thought about it, considered it from every angle, and then freed herself to act.

Putting it all Together

We have each provided unique examples of how you can use your intuitive impulses to improve your life. We both have great instincts, but our ways of interacting with and using our instincts differ. Neither way is wrong, and both produce amazing results.

Sim used her instincts to catapult her towards her future. Angie listened to her intuition to stay away from a path that would have led to an uneventful and dull life. Together, our instincts help us soar into our vision for the future, while keeping us grounded in the present moment as well.

Your intuition gives you direct access to a wealth of intelligence that greatly exceeds your conscious brain. When you shut it down or ignore it, you are depriving yourself of a form of intelligence and imagination that can help you make quantum leaps in your evolution.

How do you react to your intuition? Do you dismiss its nudges, or do you pay attention to what it tells you?

Using Instincts to Walk Through a Minefield

The first and most important thing that your instincts can do for you is warn you of danger. When we started working together, we threw ourselves into our chosen field. We travelled, we attended conferences, we networked and we met many, many people.

As you get started in entrepreneurship, you will encounter many new people, perhaps more than you've ever met before in your life. Everyone is smiling, everyone has amazing treasures to offer, and everyone is looking to help you.... right?

Not necessarily!

Sim and Angie met a lot of people, but soon, they realized that not all of those people had their best interests at heart. There are those in every field who are inauthentic or lack integrity, and your intuition will warn you of these people if you listen to it. Angie and Sim did their best to weed out these bad influencers, ensuring that only good connections entered their circle.

In the early days of their partnership, Sim and Angie attended a conference on property investing. At first glance, everything looked great, and the man who was leading the seminar to attract property investors had all the right credentials on paper. Before the presentation started, Angie walked to the washroom and almost bumped into a man as he was coming out of it. Inexplicably, the bells went off in Angie's head and she immediately thought to herself, "used car salesman." She couldn't quite put her finger on why; it could have been the nylon plaid suit, or any number of other, subtler cues. Her rational mind couldn't explain why, but her intuitive mind was sending out red-hot alerts.

Dress sense aside, the lead presenter looked promising. He was well-educated, articulate, and he had an impressive track record of successful investments, or so it seemed. His job at the seminar was to persuade potential investors to come up with $1.5 million to invest in his property ventures. Sim's intuitive flash came when she was having a conversation with the presenter about his past accomplishments. When the name of a property investor who they both knew came up, he made a scathing remark about this acquaintance, blaming the man for having robbed him of his money.

With these words, the volume of Sim's intuitive alarm bell increased tenfold, and from that moment she became highly skeptical of everything this presenter said. There was no way she could immediately check into the truth of his statements, but she couldn't ignore her strong feeling that something just wasn't right. When Sim and Angie checked in with each other and realized that they had both individually felt that something was "off," they decided to give his property venture a pass. Nonetheless, they wondered on occasion if they had made the right decision; after all, he had looked so great on paper.

A year later, Sim and Angie were surprised (or maybe not) to read in the papers that this presenter had been found guilty of fraud. It turned out that the mutual acquaintance whom he maintained had stolen his money was in fact one of his victims!

Part of learning to trust your instincts is learning to recognize people who do not mean you well, no matter how they look on the surface, while walking towards the partners that your intuition guides you to.

Metrics vs Intuition

When you are an entrepreneur, there are many decisions you can take, each of which will send you down a different path. Do you want to work with this customer or extend credit to someone new, do you wish to source from this supplier, do you invest in this particular deal or should you want to expand your company? You may conduct expensive market research but, in the end, you still have to make a decision. At this point, which path do you choose? How do you weigh analytical metrics against intuition? Do you trust your gut feelings, or let the decision be dictated by logic?

We say that, when you get an intuitive hit, don't block it out. This voice from deep within you is speaking for a reason, and it should not be ignored. When we say that you have a deep and abiding power inside you, this is what we are talking about. True success depends on your ability to listen to your inner voice.

Building a Muscle

Trusting your intuition is like building a muscle. You may start by following your instincts with risks where the stakes are relatively low. Then, as these risks pay off over time, you will learn to trust your intuition with riskier decisions.

If you are lucky enough to find a partner with whom you are in sync, your combined instincts can pack an extremely powerful punch. In our story, it was a case of 1 + 1 = 3! We are lucky to have each other to check in with, and when both our intuitive senses tell us a deal is a no-go, we listen to this unquestioningly. As the story above makes clear, it has saved us a truckload of money!

Looking Inward to Surpass Outer Limits

Look back into your past for an incident when your intuition directed you correctly down a pathway different from the one your logical mind wanted to follow.

How did you react? Did you listen to it, or did you initially ignore it and push it away? What was the result of the choice you made?

Ultimately, all limitation is self-created. We trip ourselves up saying "I can't, I won't, I'll fail" and letting fear dictate our choices, instead of focusing on a solution. Cast fear aside, and you'll find yourself able to do exactly what you need to do to succeed.

When in doubt, find the inspiration within.

As you travel down the path of entrepreneurship, you will gain comfort with your own way of moving, fighting and learning, of navigating around obstacles, and of marking new territories. There are no maps for where you are going. As such, we encourage you to be best companions with your intuition, to give it air time, because it is a part of you. Own your intuitive choices, and let them do the work they need to do.

When you decide to break away from your safety zone, your path will be significantly different from the one you traveled on before. We encourage you, at each fork on the road, to listen to your inner voice. Don't be afraid of your feelings and intuition. Instead, celebrate them, own them, and let them direct you forward to that brilliant future that is waiting for you.

Chapter 6
Hurdling Over the Bumps on the Road

The best way to treat obstacles is to use them as stepping-stones.
Laugh at them, tread on them, and let them
lead you to something better.
– Enid Blyton

Let's talk lions.

Even though they are the kings of the jungle, lions have to hunt to survive. Unlike humans, they cannot simply order a pizza or head to the grocery store. Instead, a lion needs to get up in the morning, and it needs to be faster than the slowest gazelle in the herd. It instinctively understands that, if it is not at least as fast as the slowest gazelle, it will starve to death.

There is a lesson to be taken from this. In the first place, whether you are a lion or a gazelle, you need to wake up every day fearless. The gazelle is not afraid of the lion. If it was, it would never graze on the savannah; it would instead waste away or be too defenseless to put up a fight. The instinct to live is always stronger than the fear of death so, every day, the gazelle moves to pasture. Nonetheless, it is wary, and it knows it may need to put on a burst of speed to outrun the lion.

When we think about things that slow us down, what it always boils down to is fear. We have had our own encounters with fear, but we've stared it in the face, and guess who flinched first? Not us! Although fear was addressed in Chapter 2, we bring it up again because it is by grasping the nature of fear, anxiety or worry that we can find our way around any roadblocks or obstacles.

Fortunately, we learned early on that most fear is simply not based on anything real, and the blocks we think are 'out there' are really in our minds for the most part. This has helped us develop an attitude of positive expectation, which allows us to look past our *fears* about how things are, to how they *actually* are. From there, we can follow our knowledge and passion to the appropriate action to take in any given situation. We believe that, to succeed, you have to love the journey at least as much as the destination, and that fear is no more than 'false evidence appearing real.' When you know this, life becomes really fun!

Brainstorming to Breakthrough

We had a rocky beginning in our property investing business. One of our divisions was to help families who weren't eligible for a mortgage get into home ownership within 1-3 years. Somehow we weren't making inroads, despite our best efforts. Even though Sim had previously built a multi-million dollar property portfolio, the slow start made her slightly anxious with her Rent To Own division. Had the market changed, were there too many competitors? Although she never doubted her partner's unerring instincts about investments, Angie wondered what was the spanner in the works that had them at standstill.

Then one day, Angie said, "Hell, let's go big. Let's stop playing small!" True to form, Sim decided that they should jump in with both feet. We planned a more aggressive approach. We attended networking events together, then decided to have fun with marketing and wrapped our car in decals. What better way to get the word out than through mobile advertising? It was fun, it would give us exposure 24/7 and it would definitely put an imprint on the minds of the passers-by or even the drivers in the cars behind us on the highway.

We made an appointment to get Sim's car wrapped with custom designs. When it rolled out, complete with decals, we were pumped! We had "RENT TO OWN" splashed on the side doors and across the back was a bold message saying "STOP RENTING; OWN YOUR HOME TODAY."

We drove that car everywhere – all across British Columbia, to the neighbouring province of Alberta and even across the southern border into the United States.

It was an out-of-the box approach when many other property-investing companies were relying on flyers and online ads and newspapers, but it did the trick. We started getting serious inquiries in response to our mobile billboard, and that was how we built our brand as the Rent To Own specialists in the Vancouver area.

It may not seem like a revolutionary strategy but, for us, success starts with a series of small wins, which form the foundation for the big ones to follow. When we found a way to replace anxiety with fun and joy, we fell in love with our business again.

Overcoming Common Blocks Faced by Entrepreneurs

Most of us can uncover some of our core subconscious worries with relatively little effort, and it is often surprising how irrational they are. If you find yourself constantly held back by imaginary limitations, it's really worth taking the time to dig up the roots of your anxieties, perhaps with the help of a trusted coach, mentor or advisor, as those worries and anxieties are usually attached to some limiting beliefs that may stem from your early life experiences. When you see how irrational your fears are, it becomes much easier to let them go, and this is the key to developing the positive attitude you need to succeed. Our fears are rooted in our unconscious thought patterns, but they can't survive in the light of awareness.

So, what's the most effective way to transcend the common blocks faced by budding entrepreneurs? We'll look at 3 examples that resonate for us:

- **Lack of self-belief**
  When you have a really grand vision, this can trigger the basic lack of self-worth that most humans seem to have. The way to tackle this is to work on small victories every day, in order to build your confidence in your own capabilities. We said in the previous chapter that intuition is a muscle that needs building through frequent exercise, and so is the ability to embrace success. When you break down your big dream into small steps, not only does this help you take action daily, but it also helps you hold your vision more lightly, so that something even greater than you can imagine has room to come through. Once you get used to having success internally, it's easy for the universe to bring you big wins!

- **Needing to be perfect**
  A wise man once said, 'don't sweat the small stuff,' and by

the same token, don't let perfectionism hold you back! Don't lose sleep over needing to have the perfect logo or website. If we had waited for the perfect advertising strategy, we would never have gone ahead with our car decals. Some people may turn up their noses at that strategy because they think it's cheesy, but what matters to us is that it worked. We knew there were people out there who needed our brand of property financing and our special creative tactics, and we had to get in front of them in any way we could. We know we can always upgrade our publicity tactics over time. Good and profitable is much more effective than perfect with zero business.

- **You don't have the chops**
  You probably have heard several versions of this. You don't have a degree in business, so what do you know about investing? You are not experienced enough, and you don't have a lot of starting capital either. Do you even know how to put together a business plan? In response to these criticisms, we say that the world is full of knowledge – all you have to do is reach out for it. Find a mentor, and enroll in classes and workshops that appeal to you. We found a partner we could trust in each other, someone who would offer a different point of view, someone we could learn from, and with whom we could safely test the durability of our ideas.

The Fringe Benefits of Failure

Many dreams never manifest because the person is afraid of failure. Many businesses stay small because the entrepreneur is afraid of failure. We can't stress this enough — it is okay to fail because you learn more from your failures than you do from your successes, and we lean on the words of one of the world's most successful female writers to explain why it's fine to embrace failure.

In her commencement speech in Harvard in 2008, JK Rowling said, "So why do I talk about the benefits of failure? Simply because failure meant a stripping away of the inessential. I stopped pretending to myself that I was anything other than what I was, and began to direct all my energy into finishing the only work that mattered to me...... Failure gave me an inner security that I had never attained by passing examinations. Failure taught me things about myself that I could have learned no other way. I discovered that I had a strong will, and more discipline than I had suspected; I also found out that I had friends whose value was truly above the price of rubies."

Need we say more?

Taking Action Creates Forward Momentum

Remember that action is energy at work. You can be bogged down by indecision or uncertainty or you can power forward. The trick is to choose positivity and expansion every time an obstacle or a limitation attempts to dominate your awareness; this is the cornerstone of a winning attitude.

Did you know that it is impossible to feel positive and grateful and worry at the same time? One of the simplest and most empowering practices you can do is to find something to dip into gratitude for, every time you find yourself vulnerable to anxiety or if you are stumped for a solution. Commit to living from gratitude; the universe will reward you greatly for it!

Take a moment to think about which thoughts and emotions you are feeding. The laws of physics tell us that everything is energy, and this holds true emotionally as well. What are you feeding with your time and energy? When you feel stalled by a problem, you have a choice about whether you are going to feed the stalemate or replace it with love, and gratitude is a great place to start.

Self-doubt can be destructive and it can make imaginary mountains out of anthills. The greatest enemy of self-doubt is positivity, so give yourself a pep talk. What you need to do is remind yourself that ultimately there is no such thing as failure. You need to understand that your worth is infinite as a human being, and that the universe offers obstacles out of love for you, to support your learning. We are never given more than we can handle, but the choice to prevail, or not, is always yours. When you love yourself, it is much easier to summon the inner reserves required to reach your goals, come what may. These reserves are always there, but self-love makes them much more accessible.

Affirmations to Empower Yourself with Love

Affirmations are, at their core, positive statements that you feed yourself.

Your inner critic will tell you that you'll come across as foolish or delusional when you offer yourself love. To this we say that the more resistance something elicits in you, the more powerful the result will likely be once you break down the resistance and make a connection. It's been our experience that there are few daily practices with more power to transform your life than this. The way we see it, you must put yourself at the centre of your life, because if you don't believe in yourself, who will?

These affirmations will help you out immensely, even if it feels uncomfortable to do them in the beginning. Let us help you, so that you too can become a strong individual. We know it is possible because we have done it, and we have a vision for you, just as you have a vision for yourself.

Here are some possibilities:

*I am unstoppable.

*My unique purpose and vision have infinite value.

* I deserve all the good that's coming to me.

*I am never given more than I can handle.

*I love, and I am loved.

*I am born to win.

* Solutions come to me easily and effortlessly.

These simple affirmations can have a profound positive effect on your ability to move forward. The more you fill yourself with self-love, the easier it becomes to perform better, and the more you will expect of yourself and the universe.

The Most Powerful Weapon is Positivity

Remember that, when you rid yourself of limitations, you need fill the empty space with powerful positive emotions like optimism and gratitude. This is important, because nature abhors a vacuum. When you clear your inner space of embedded limiting attitudes, a vacuum is created. When you fill it consciously, rather than unconsciously, with joy, gratitude, adventure and a can-do attitude, all good things will find their way to you.

If you want to grow and excel as a person and as an entrepreneur, you need to feed the inner qualities that will carry you to your goals, like your ambition and your strength and the power of reason. Like a sunflower following the sun, you must always choose to look for love, potential and promise. When you do, you will be ready to claim your own rightful place in the sun.

* * *

Success Story from the Frontlines #4: Tahnee Lam, M.A.
Program director and senior consultant, New Step Consultation
Services Inc. and New Step Consultation (International) Ltd.

Success can be defined in many ways. To me, success is the satisfaction experienced through conquering obstacles while following my life's path with passion.

In 2002, autism was just another disorder I had to study for my exam. At that time, I never imagined that this condition would have such an impact on the next 10 years of my life. In 2003, I started work as a part-time behavioural interventionist, and my very first client was a four year old boy who was diagnosed with autism spectrum disorder. He was only able to use simple words to communicate his wants and needs, he didn't make much eye contact and he displayed aggressive behaviour at times. During the first few months, he pulled my hair, bit my neck and scratched my arms a number of times. The situation remained tolerable—that is, until I had to run an intensive toilet-training program with him. During the program, he would sit on my lap and use me as a "human potty." I was utterly disgusted; after 2 weeks of training, he showed no sign of being toilet trained. Just when I was about to quit the training, he came up to me and said: "I want pee pee." Tears of joy poured down my face and I knew that was the moment when I discovered my path in life.

In my early 20s, I focused on just (barely) passing my courses and so it took me almost 6 years to complete my undergraduate degree. However, once I had figured out that my passion was working with special needs students, I studied and worked full force. For the next 5 years, until I turned 26, I frequently worked from 9:00am to 8:00pm, 6-7 days a week. Then there was a period of a year when I studied for my graduate degree and two other professional certificates while still working full-time. I also had my share of challenges; for example, dealing with a boss who forced me to continue working after I was physically hurt by a student. Although the stress was enormous, I managed to build the confidence necessary to pursue the next step of my career—starting my own company.

I named my company "New Step" because I hoped to provide new steps for every child in order for them to reach their fullest potential. Starting the company wasn't difficult, but increasing the revenue each year was a huge challenge since the services I provide are quite atypical. Without an office, I dragged my big suitcase of toys to the public library rooms that I had rented to conduct my social skills therapy sessions. For the first 3 years, I took every opportunity to promote my business, spending numerous unpaid hours putting flyers up and never turning down an unpaid speaking job for parent support groups, clinics and schools. After a year, I had gained enough students to have a team of staff and my very own office.

After more than 10 years of blood, sweat and tears, I had turned myself into a woman able to maintain a successful and meaningful business. Looking back, I would not have been able to succeed without putting every possible effort towards my dream. To fulfill a dream, simply making plans in your head is never enough; you will need to work exceptionally hard to pave the road towards that dream. Looking back now, I would not have been able to succeed without following my chosen path in life with passion, paying my dues and seizing every opportunity that came my way.

Chapter 7
Dream Out Loud!

Throw your dreams into space like a kite,
and you do not know what it will bring back,
a new life, a new friend, a new love, a new country.

– Anaïs Nin

When it comes to dreams, we have a simple motto: If you have the imagination to dream big, you have the capacity to make your dream real.

Children have it right. When they wish upon a star, they don't immediately cancel out their fondest wishes with doubt. They don't think to themselves that the dreams are impossible. All they know is that they are driven by some inexplicable urge. Something that feels good bubbles up from within them and they aspire and thrive on the essence of that feeling. They don't get all twisted and knotted up with the "hows" and the "whys."

Then we grow up.

When Sim was a little girl, she wanted nothing more than to be a policewoman, when she wasn't orchestrating her convoy of toy semi-trucks in the backyard. She wanted the badge, she wanted the authority, and she wanted to use all of it to keep the people in her community safe and sound. When Angie was a little girl, she could never settle on one dream. She wanted to be a doctor and scientist, to find a cure for cancer and for peanut allergies, and a photographer, to capture the wonders of the world, and sometimes she wanted to be all 3.

The dream to be a doctor had so gripped Angie that, even before she mastered writing out the alphabet, she would sneak into her parents' room, take out the expensive notepad and hide under the desk to practice her signature for when she had to sign off on reports and prescriptions. This was well before she learned how to spell her name, but she felt so strongly about her dream that she decided to put into practice at a tender age what she thought she might need as an adult.

The problem is that, when we grow up, we suppress our dreams. We allow what we deem as adult responsibilities, to nurture a career and care for family, to take priority. And we bury our dreams, lest they become too disruptive.

Dreams change. What we longed for as a child may assume a different shape when we grow in years. But if you look closely, you may find that something still connects what we desire to achieve as an adult and what we dreamed of as a kid. Sim is not in the police force and Angie is not a doctor, but note the connecting thread – they still yearn to help and heal others, except they are now using different modalities.

The Power of Your Dreams

The truth of it is that we do ourselves an injustice when we stop believing in the power and the magic of our dreams. Dreams can be everything, yet they can be as fleeting as a soap bubble. If you are without a dream, life seems monotonous. You're no better than a hamster running perpetually on the wheel, because there is nothing to look forward to. Just more of the same. If you have a dream and nothing else, all you have is a clever imagination and nothing more besides.

What dreams need is power behind them. They require belief, energy and strength, and they demand that those powerful forces be applied to their completion. That is the only way you can bring the magic of your imagination to life. To make that leap from within to without, from inner wishful thinking to outer life, from a doodle on a napkin to bricks and mortar, you need to do something. And it starts with dreaming out loud in a big way.

Our dream was to write a book that would inspire other women to pursue their dreams the way we have. Here we are, seeing the words sprawl across the page. From dream to reality, it took effort and it took courage, but it took less than you probably think.

Meanwhile during the process of completing our book, we discovered the potency of dreaming. It was once we gave ourselves permission to go powerfully in the direction of our dreams – in this specific case, co-authoring a book – that there was more power that we could tap into to bring about all the other dreams that we had.

For Angie, the manifestation of the book blew open the lid that had held down a secret dream, to be a public speaker on the global stage. As the book took heft and weight, she found herself becoming more and more comfortable with the thought, the possibility and now the probability, of becoming a motivational speaker to inspire other women.

This is a dream that Angie has in common with Sim, to galvanize other women into taking control of their own destinies. There was a time in the past when Sim was reluctant to voice her dreams. She was afraid that she might be found wanting if she fell short of the achievement. However, the Sim of today says "Who cares what others think!" She knows she has a strong support system, and the accomplishment of her other dreams has given her confidence to knock it out of the park in whatever she does next. Her family will always cheer on her dreams, and her business partner, Angie, is always in her corner.

Are you ready to dream BIG? Are you ready to make your dreams a reality?

We want you to dream out loud, and we know that there has never been a better time for you to begin than this very moment.

Claim Ownership of Your Dreams

Here's the thing that we will never understand about dreams:

Some people are self-conscious about their dreams. We don't like to stereotype but, in our experience, it is far more often women are who have to bury or suppress their dreams. They shrug them off, call them unimportant, and never want to discuss them. They let becoming a soccer Mum take precedence, and they shelve their dreams for another day. If that describes you, the best advice we can give you is to stop putting your dreams aside, because another day often never comes, unless you actively work towards it.

Be wonderfully proud of your dreams. They come from the depths of you, and they are part of what makes you extraordinary, of what gives you the power to live your life in your own special way. If we were shy to talk about our dreams, we would never be where we are now. We would never be in a place where we can speak confidently about our lives or the successful businesses that we share.

We Began with a Dream and a Vision

Sim's dream first came from wanting to help her parents. In redefining her life after emerging from the abusive relationship, Sim took a long look at what was going on, and made it her dream to build an empire that would include businesses in transportation and real estate. She was fired by a deep, yearning desire to help her family so they didn't have to live from pay cheque to pay cheque, but she knew that this could only be accomplished by focusing herself first.

After the bankruptcy, Sim's father earned money by driving a truck, but when Sim conceived the idea of starting a trucking company together, they both leapt at the possibility. From the germ of an idea to a multi-million dollar company took just 3 years. The company now involves her whole family. Her brothers are in sales, her father in dispatch, and her mother handles administration while Sim stays in charge of everything else to keep the business flowing. Just as importantly, she is helping her employees earn a good living that supports their own families in a comfortable life.

Sim saw how Rent to Own had put her family back into a real home. It was through such a home ownership program that they could own the roof over their heads sooner rather than later. Sim was deeply grateful for such a program, and when she shared this with Angie, she realized that they had touched on something profoundly important.

Bringing a Vision to Life

When this happened, we realized that we had also discovered a business opportunity that matched all our values. One of our dreams in business is to help families get into homes of their own, no matter how much is stacked against them. They may have poor credit scores and insufficient down payment to meet the hurdles laid down by the banks and mortgage lenders. However, we believe everyone deserves a home, and every time we move a family into their own house, we feel we've done the right thing. We were right to dream; if we had not, there would be a lot of people left out on the fringes, who would not be as comfortable and as happy as they are today.

Rent to Own is just one of the seeds in our big vision, although it is one that we deeply cherish. We want to strengthen and expand our residential, commercial and industrial real estate portfolio in Canada and globally.

We all begin as a dream, in the minds of our parents. So when it comes down to it, we are all made of dreams. When you disallow yourself to dream, you are stacking the deck against you, not anyone else. Not only that, you are robbing yourself of your natural birthright. Without our dreams, we are no better than drones. Your dream is what gives you the inspiration; it's the kickstarter that turns wishful thinking into possibility and into reality.

Act It Out!

If you are not working on your dreams, they're pointless. We don't mean to be rude or cruel, but that's the bottom and the top of it.

Angie and Sim saw their mission as making a world a better place. They realized that, if they didn't plan, strategize and take action towards their joint dream, it would be as fluffy as cotton candy that melts in the heat of reality.

You need to act on your dreams now. There are simply no excuses. There is absolutely nothing standing in your way of stepping a little closer to your dream right now. Maybe the naysayers are beating their drums and droning, "It is too hard. It takes years of training! But it takes thousands of dollars!" Who are you going to pay heed to? Strangers or even well-meaning friends who are not living your life in your shoes, or yourself?

Just remember that every step you take, no matter how small, how seemingly insignificant, draws you one step closer. With every decision and act made towards fulfilling your dream, you are becoming a doer, one who is making the world a much better place to live in. As multi-book author Sarah Ban Breathnach says, "The world needs dreamers and the world needs doers. But above all, the world needs dreamers who do."

Finding Others, Reaching Out

One thing that Sim and Angie have always known is that they can depend on each other. They always have each other's back. As much as they defend their common business interests with gusto, they defend each other with greater ferocity.

Women entrepreneurs have a tough go of it. We are still very much in the minority and, in some circles, our dreams are laughed at simply because we are women working in men's fields. That is why both of us want to reach out. When we were just getting started, we remembered how a woman speaker would always get our attention, and whenever we spoke to one, we were welcomed as if we were sisters.

The common myth is that women are naturally self-interested, and competitive with each other. However, the more we put ourselves out there, the more we find ourselves involved in amazing relationships with other female entrepreneurs. We are making a difference, and we are not alone. In some ways, we never were!

As you are getting your dream off of the ground, you can do it alone, but it could take you an immeasurable length of time, and the burden of time demanded of you could be intimidating or overwhelming. Instead, what we want you to do is reach out. Your dream is nothing that cannot be achieved, and now we will prove it to you.

If you have a dream, put it out there and allow people to give you ideas, resources and help. Women want to see other women succeed, and it is in doing this that you will find yourself and your own dreams. Look for someone who can help you, and be willing to move forward with the kind of hope that you carry in your heart.

Exercise in the Right to Dream

It is not always easy to reach out. We understand that. If you are naturally shy, if you are nervous, and if you have had dreams crash and burn before this, you need to be willing to do it.

Right now, go straight to a mirror, and look yourself in the eye. Look and really see yourself. Look at what a strong human being you are. You have suffered, but you have emerged triumphant. You deserve to pursue your dream as much as anyone else, and you have the power to move mountains if you want to.

Say to yourself, "I deserve to dream."

Say, "I deserve my dream."

Say "My dream is powerful!"

After that, state what your dream is. It might feel a little harrowing to hear the sound of your own voice say something so boldly or so strongly, but it is necessary. If you cannot say your dream to yourself, who are you ever going to say it to? Who are you ever going to be able to speak to about it? Unless you can speak your dream and look yourself straight in the eye, you may find the way forward tough going.

Speaking your dream out loud gives you purpose, clarity and a point of focus. That very act also creates ripples in the creative energies that turn dreams into reality and, by claiming your dream with pride and courage, you are gathering to you the energies of momentum and manifestation that help make it real.

Pond or Ocean

There's more to dreams than simply writing words on paper and speaking to yourself. Dreams deserve to be brought into the world, and in order for them to be realized, you have to be strong, you have to believe that you are powerful.

You cannot flinch, thinking that you can simply will your dream into being. You need to find your own strength, and then you need to put it into harness. Focus, commitment, action – those are the next steps that will follow naturally.

Are you ready to make a big difference to your own world? Are you ready to have your dream be a reality?

Don't shy away from the possibility of your dream. Don't balk at the size of it. Instead, celebrate that you are worthy of something big. Next, make the right choices that support your dream. You will gravitate towards the most dominant of your dreams, the one you pay most attention to, so make sure you dream BIG!

From Dodinsky's *In The Garden of Thought* comes this lovely, whimsical but unerringly accurate quote: "If others want to define you, don't linger in their pond. Swim away from their ignorance and find your ocean."

Crowded pond or in the vast ocean of possibility? Which do you choose?

Chapter 8
Walking the Tightrope of Work-Life Balance

Love yourself but also realize that you have a lifetime of work to better yourself in all aspects.

– Angie Chik

Your work is important, and it is very much a part of you, but right here and right now, we are telling you that you are not defined just by your work. You are not just an entrepreneur or a businesswoman. You are an artist, an author, a mountaineer, a mother, a daughter, a significant other. You are a multi-faceted person. Like a raw gem being polished, sawn and designed by an exacting master cutter, you are being shaped by each experience that you go through. That means that, if you dedicate your focus only to working for financial success and status, you are depriving yourself of wholeness, completeness and authenticity.

The Hyper Superwoman

Women today have opportunities in education, careers and spouses that were not available to our grandmothers, but this embarrassment of riches has created a burden for the modern woman. Just because we can now do anything, we feel we must do everything. We expect ourselves to be perfect in everything we do – we have to be tough and firm at the negotiating table and well-manicured and glamorous after a long day at the office. Does the fault lie with us? Have we internalized this phenomenon of the Superwoman, and are we breaking our backs to be better than our peers, that is, other women?

Is Work-Life Balance Unachievable?

According to the Canadian Mental Health Association, 53% of Canadians report that they are overloaded from pressures associated with work, family, home, friends, physical health, volunteer service and community. Even the technological marvels that are supposed to have made life easier – internet, computer and smart phones – have in fact blurred the lines between home and work. How many of you check work email when you are at home, out at dinner with your friends or at your gym? These lifestyle changes have imposed upon us the delusion that we must be available 24/7 to our work and, as entrepreneurs, to our own business.

Work-life balance differs for everyone. What may be considered a life in balance for us may not work for you. Nonetheless, when you are out of balance, you most certainly become aware of it. Depression, chronic fatigue and anxiety, focus on surviving rather than thriving – do these sound familiar? We flirted with some of these symptoms briefly but, fortunately, we pulled back from the work-life conflict before its effects dug too deep into our lives and our souls.

Full Steam Forward

We established a schedule, which required that we were up at dawn; after carving time for self-development, it was work, work, work, with no holds barred. After several months of this relentless schedule of living and breathing business, we found we were getting too serious. The laughs were few and far between. Angie was getting tired much faster than before and became far too serious. She just didn't know how not to work and didn't know when to stop, fuelled by ambition, competitiveness and a type A personality, which wanted to arrive at the destination yesterday.

It was Sim who was more sensitized to the dangers of imbalance. She has taken her past learning moments and turned them into positive learning experiences. It is so important to take certain experiences and events in your life and turn them into knowledge gained instead of calling them mistakes.

At age 24, Sim knew, from skin to bone, she could do it all over again. She recognized that, by deliberately restructuring her life for optimal balance, no matter how penalizing and massive the immediate costs, she would be able to marshal her inner forces and energies for a bright and successful future. Having repositioned herself internally for strength, Sim became a warrior woman, determined to break down all barriers and start her new business ventures.

Her family is now living the comfortable life they were previously denied. Additionally, she created balance within her life. She now focuses on all levels of her life; health, family, relationships, business, learning, enjoyment, and much more. Sim's words of wisdom; "Each day is a new day with challenges and victories; however, don't stop living the life you desire. Remember, balance is key."

With all that behind her, when she launched a new partnership with Angie, Sim was well aware of the pitfalls when work became all-consuming.

She recognized that the time had come for both of them to make significant changes.

Checking in for a Retune

We didn't arrive at the epiphany in minutes. In fact, it was a slow process of self-discovery. We came to understand that the success of the business rested on our shoulders, but if we weren't firing on all cylinders – physical and emotional health, family, hobbies and interests, friendships, exercise and play – we weren't going to be as strong and as present as a successful business needed us to be.

Small Wins through Time Management

We want it all, so we have to prioritize what is important to us. We came to understand that work-life balance doesn't mean that we allocate our time equally across all portions of our life. Instead, what matters is quality over quantity, and not cramming anything and everything into our limited time.

Are you one of those who find getting ready in the morning a real battle? Are you flustered by the time you get to work because you waited 20 minutes for your morning Starbucks and need at least half an hour of mindless tasks before you can start to be productive? Before you know it, your day has gone and you've accomplished very little.

Instead of starting the day with morning mayhem, we took steps to prepare the night before for the day ahead. And we did so with the intention to have a fruitful day that would focus on our core competencies, and accomplishments that would get us closer to our goals.

We looked through our notes and refreshed ourselves on any meetings that would take place the next day so that everything would go as smoothly as we could help it. We chose our clothes for the day so that, rather than finding a tear in our jackets just as we were going out of the door, we saved ourselves precious time by investing just a few minutes the night before.

We knew of a couple of successful business women who would lay out their jogging clothes down to the hair ties and pins the night before, position their shoes and a pair of socks right at the door, so they wouldn't lose time or give in to excuses the next morning. All these little steps don't consume a lot of time, at most 10-20 minutes, but you get hours of productivity in return.

We came to understand that, while we may work a 10-hour or 12-hour day or more, it wasn't really 10 or 12 hours of time we could control. As the day goes by, there are more and more demands on our time, from customers, from suppliers, from investment prospects. Unexpected events butt into our time at work. Knowing that's how a day normally transpires, we decided to allocate our morning hours towards strategizing and making decisions on matters of the highest priority.

Reconnecting with the Things You Love in Me-Time.

At the same time, we deliberately created me-time to nurture ourselves. For Angie, going for a walk or having play time with her pet chinchilla and her dog was crucial. She also discovered that she had given up something that was deeply meaningful and fulfilling to her – during an earlier darker period, Angie had given up on playing the piano, a pursuit she had loved, from when she was too short to press the pedals, through to adulthood. At the piano, absorbed by the golden, lyrical tones that were produced, Angie could escape from her thoughts and the world around her.

When Angie recognized that depriving herself of her music was detrimental to her sense of wellbeing and her self-esteem, she resumed playing the piano. Classical and Baroque music created a sanctuary of peace around her, and when her mind was sufficiently quiet, her creativity would bubble up. She had an innate gift. When she reconnected with her love of and artistry at the piano, she gave herself the beauty and the energy she sorely needed.

World travel is Sim's all-time favourite. She is nurtured by exploring unknown corners of the love, of learning the history of far-off and foreign places. She loves watching documentaries from which she derives much information because, to Sim, knowledge is power. In addition to connecting with her soul through the music of Tabla, Sim loves spending time with her purebreed German Shepherd, Lucky. She finds joy every day in simple pleasures like taking a walk in the park and sharing laughs with a close friend, and she adds meaning to her life by taking daily steps to improve herself and boost her happiness.

Here's something else to think about: Although the world we live in now has enabled us to connect with people and events all over the world, in truth, we have never been more disconnected with each other. Take some time out to have some real facetime, and not over rely on the "Facetime" on your mobile devices. By this we mean that you should connect in person, to look your friend in the eyes and truly enjoy each other's company without simultaneously thumbing through your tweets or text messages. Be fully present; you may be surprised by how fulfilling a real encounter is, as opposed to a Facebook "like" or a series of texts or tweets.

Audit Your Time

If you are one of those people who fret about always running out of time, do a time audit for a few days or a work week. Notice how you spend your time at work and on weekends. When you look at the results of your audit, look to the following:

- Can you redistribute your time better?
- What can you eliminate, reduce or delegate?
- What are you spending your time on that you don't really enjoy?
- Are there people who are a drain on your energy that you could do without?
- When are you most energetic?
- Where do you waste your time most?

Keep a lookout for anything or anyone that causes a repetitive drain on your time, be it work systems, technology or people. Address and fix these time drains one by one. You may have to fix them, change them or completely do away with them to free up time for more productive uses.

You may require a digital detox over the weekend. Step away from the constant stimulation of technology. Ignore the pings and rings and the frequent alerts, peel your eyes off the screens on your phones, iPad, computers, TV and other devices. Be aware of the effects that time online has on your relationships and on your life, and mindfully and deliberately learn to have some me-time without artificial stimulation. Try disconnecting in order to reconnect!

Likewise, when it comes to sleep, do away with technological distractions. Sleep is when the body recharges itself, and if you whittle your sleep hours away by browsing or checking emails on your smart phone while in bed, you are doing yourself a disservice. When you settle in for the night, power down your mobile device. If you rely on the smartphone's alarm, turn the phone to airplane mode.

Balance Begins with Honouring Yourself

Sim uses the Life Balance Wheel, a coaching tool to keep herself in check. As she is passionate about helping others, she knows that she can be a model of inspiration to others only when her own life is happy.

Think of it as a pie-chart divided into 9 segments:
- Work
- Money
- Relationships
- Helping Others
- Spiritual Fulfillment

- Love
- Health
- Learning
- Fun & Enjoyment

The Wheel of Life is a snapshot of how happy you are and how balanced your life is. It reminds you that you are a many-faceted person, and starving one part of yourself inevitably has unpleasant consequences for the other bits of you. Similarly, improvements made in any segment creates a ripple effect, and the increased satisfaction, contentment and fulfillment you feel spills over into the other areas.

When you are just getting your business off of the ground, it is very easy to think that you need to give it everything you have. However, as a very wise person said, the world doesn't stop for work or fun.

You are a complete person. That means that not everything that you need to live and function as a whole, passionate and successful person can be found in your business. Don't think of work-life balance as a win-lose proposition. Instead, think of making changes that can positively impact the rest of your life. Everyone can do this; you intuitively know what those changes need to be. Take small steps and make sure you are being real to your own values.

A Little Extra about the Wheel

Getting to know the balance wheel can help you stay on top of things, so we thought we would dive deeper into how it works. If one area of the wheel is on fire, it will spread, and that means you must be willing to tend to each.

Work: You know all about this! Work is something that must happen, but it cannot be the only thing going on in your life. Get your work life taken care of, and then go home. Decide how many hours you are going to work, and then stick with it! It is all about adhering firmly to your schedule.

Money: Devote some of your time to managing your money. Some people think that this is a segment that can be folded into work, but the two are not very similar at all. When you work, you are making money. When you have the money, you need to decide what to do with it. Invest your cash, expand your business, or look for other ways to make your money grow.

Relationships: When many people think of relationships, they think of romantic relationships, but there is more to life than romance. You have relationships with everyone important in your life, and you must take the time to nurture them. Make time with your friends, bond with your family, and make the time for all kinds of love! Author and psychiatrist Edward

Hallowell said, "Never worry alone." We are all prone to worrying now and again, but you don't have to do it alone. As business partners and friends, we have each other to bounce off ideas, to halve the load of worries and anxieties, and to share and celebrate moments of laughter and joy with.

Helping Others: Helping others, in many ways, is simply helping yourself. Reach out to people who need a hand, whether they are close or whether they are strangers. You can learn from helping others, and you never know when it will yield an important opportunity.

Spiritual Fulfilment: There is more to this world than what we can sense. Take care of your spiritual needs. Whether this means inwardly connecting with yourself or simply meditating on the universe, make the time to recharge and find inner peace.

Love: Love who you want to love, and show them that you love them. Let them show you that they love you as well. Unless you are making time for this, you are missing out!

Health: A healthy body feeds a healthy mind. Exercise, eat well, and take care of your body. It's the only one you have! Without good health, everything else – a thriving business, fame and fortune – pales into insignificance.

Learning: One of the most important things that you can do as a person is to learn. When you learn, you are keeping yourself sharp and you are staying informed and well-rounded in your interests. Knowledge is power; there is no such thing as a wasted education. Take every opportunity to deepen and widen your knowledge base.

Fun and Enjoyment: Kick back and have some fun. Some people think of this as a reward for working hard, but it should in fact be a natural part of your life. Getting the right fun in your life keeps you excited, and it prevents a day to day drag.

Sit down and make a list with each of the wedges of the balance wheel listed on them carefully.

Write down what you are going to do to nurture each of these parts as you move forward. Some people dismiss this as fluffy or silly, but give it a try. This exercise is all about mindfulness; as you write down these things, we guarantee that you are going to start nodding along.

Your life is your own, and of course, so is what you do with it. Take a look at this wheel and think about what you are missing out on and what you need to be thinking about improving.

Helping Yourself to Help Others

Throughout this chapter, we have outlined suggestions and anecdotes that point to the importance of self-care for an optimal, balanced life. For those who may feel that self-care is selfish, we argue that it is instead selfish not to take care of yourself and to expect others to do so.

Without self-care, you may end up resenting that you are helping others succeed when you are not getting to where you want to be. It is only when you make the decisions and choices that honour the deepest reaches of your soul that you can reach out and make a positive contribution to the world.

By first leading a rich and purposeful life, you will in turn be able to inspire others to do the same. Self-care is a precious gift. When you give it to yourself, you are gifting it to others too. Like in all things, the transformation begins firstly with you.

* * *

Success Story from the Frontlines #5: Vindy Teja
Life Coach

I was a focused teen whose goals were to do well in school, play a lot of sports, have fun, attend university, become a lawyer, and meet a great guy to marry and start a family with. All of that came to fruition. There was no reason for it not to, especially given that I was a happy, motivated and well-adjusted kid with loving and encouraging parents and great friends, and little drama in my life.

Like many, my life had challenges and blessings. For example, after I was married, I moved about the country, mostly for my husband's professional training. I adapted my career plan and worked as a director of legal career development. Shortly after I prematurely lost my father to pancreatic cancer, my husband and I experienced serious fertility issues. We pursued treatment and a couple of years later we were blessed with the birth of our daughter.

We got pregnant again a year later, only to learn mid-way through the pregnancy that our baby had a severe heart defect that would likely result in his death at birth. After much research and deliberation, I made the most difficult decision of my life: terminate the pregnancy. Nine months later I underwent fertility treatment again, unsuccessfully. Despite all of this, we knew we were blessed to have our daughter, and we never lost sight of that.

A month later, my husband separated from me, in what I call a cross between a Twilight Zone and Jerry Springer episode. The circumstances were shocking, and the personal and family damage were lasting. The end result: I was separated, with a 2-year old child, and unemployed. I had given up my legal career years earlier to support my husband's career and our parenting goals. I was devastated, stressed, and ill-equipped for the drama, not to mention the long, costly and emotionally draining divorce proceedings. I questioned everything I had come to believe about people, family, relationships, and life.

Although so much had happened to me, I was determined not to be angry, bitter, or broke. I made it a conscious goal to expand myself and take responsibility for creating a balanced life for me and my daughter. I became a certified life coach, so that I could integrate and use my knowledge, and life experiences to assist others in their journey. Self-development also yielded other important life results for me: I developed my physical fitness further, helped create a successful and nourishing book club, traveled regularly, and participated actively in my daughter's absolute love of music and dance.

My advice to my "fellow sisters" on their journey is to keep their heads up and do the following:

- *Practice effort with ease: be intentional, work hard, and stay focused but avoid becoming too attached to the results. Life is ever-changing after all.*
- *Approach all circumstances, both negative and positive, with a view to learning as much as you can. Life is an amazing and interactive learning tool.*
- *Don't take things personally. Staying a victim to your pain will rob you of the beauty life has to offer.*

Chapter 9
Embrace Yourself!

You are imperfect, permanently and inevitably flawed.

And you are beautiful.

– Amy Bloom

As we've taken you on this journey, we've done our best to tell you how to succeed and how to excel at your passion. This chapter brings all of that together, and the surprising revelation is that the key to success has always been you!

You yourself are a treasure, and when you succeed (note it's WHEN, not if) you are the one who shot for the stars and came away with a huge pocketful. What a rush it is to break free of boundaries and to dip into the unlimited potential that exists within you. At this moment, as you are reading this, you may be working hard towards success. You will get somewhere, but you will never uncover your truest potential if you don't embrace yourself. At the same time, you may pull off great accomplishments but if you do so only from guilt and obligation or from will power, you are going to run out of steam. To create a sustainable, committed positive impact, what you do must involve all parts of you, the light and the dark, and be sourced in your core purpose and values.

Creating an identity that rests on the core of who you are will shift your life in wondrous and miraculous ways. Both of us will advise you that, when you are setting sail for your own distant shore, you are the only captain, navigator or sailor who can get you there. Don't torture yourself trying to be someone you are not. The only role you want for yourself is the role you deem best for yourself.

The point we are making is that it all begins with you, the discovery of you and the embrace of you. This is the message that Sim wants to share. She wants to assure women, who may be caught up in a variety of predicaments. Whether you feel forestalled by sacrifices made for family, or have incurred costly mistakes that resulted in devastating financial failures, or are being bogged down by relationship problems, you have it within you to set yourself free. Freedom isn't necessarily dropping everything and walking away from it all, though that is one option. But freedom is also freedom of choice, to choose to believe that you are not defined by your mistakes and that your mistakes are not personal flaws but lessons to prepare you for greatness.

You have all you need within you to thrive; the seeds of success are already in you. Once you trust and embrace yourself, you will harness your brilliance to be a light to others who may struggle in an uncertain world.

The two of us could not be enjoying our level of success if it wasn't for our determination and persistence. We have mis-stepped but we kept our focus on where we wanted to go, not where we didn't. We saw our challenges as spurs toward growth, not growing pains, and we hope that our stories will inspire you to claim your personal power to not be the same as everyone but to be uniquely, unquestioningly and courageously You.

To get to the top of your game, to be the best version of yourself, there are 5 main areas that you need to attend to:

Self-Esteem and Insecurities

All of us have insecurities. Whether they were formed during childhood or when our feelings were hurt, these insecurities act like little blocks to our growth. Have you been in a situation where everything was coasting along and you were doing really well, and a little nagging voice pipes up to say, "It can't last, this is too good to be true?" This happens because somewhere, languishing in the dark aspects of you, is a message that you are not good enough, you are not deserving enough.

It is only by embracing these concealed and insecure parts of yourself that you can step into greatness. Without doing so, you'll drive through life like a driver who alternately puts her foot on the pedal and then on the brake. You'll accelerate and when the going gets good, your insecurities pop up, prompting you to step firmly on the brake. No one is born perfect, and by bringing consciousness to the parts of yourself that hide in the dark, you are making yourself more whole than you were before.

Angie always had trouble expressing herself in school, especially during class participation in her earlier days. Each year her elementary school reports would say that she was a great student but should speak up more and be more interactive in class. She couldn't sustain eye-contact in a conversation with others as a young girl. Her fear of speaking up and getting attention left her missing out on opportunities to make great points and contribute to discussion topics that she was very interested in. She always felt a barrier that held her back, and she knew that it was her own mind telling her that she would say something stupid or irrelevant if she spoke out in class. Although the majority of things she wanted to say made perfect sense and were critical points to bring up in discussions, her insecurity got the best of her. Each time she'd sat long enough in her chair at her desk, while her heart pounded away, and she finally mustered enough courage to commit to speaking aloud, class discussion would be over.

As a little girl, Angie knew that this particular fear, this big insecurity, was getting in the way but, luckily, she needed only to look to her mom to get some inspiration on how to be more forward and expressive with her thoughts and feelings. Angie saw her mom as a tough, independent, intelligent, outspoken and perfect role model for her. During the times when Angie was insecure about being the tallest girl in her class, her mother would tell her own stories about how, despite being heads and shoulders above the average woman in Hong Kong, she would stand tall and be proud of it in high heels.

Because of Angie's mother's personality, attitude, thinking, and influence, Angie slowly shaped herself into a more independent thinker and speaker who consciously chose to surround herself with similar individuals to further minimize her insecurities and to develop and strengthen her traits, where Sim is the prime example of someone who really assisted in getting Angie out of her own mental obstacles.

When you are willing to cast a light on both the bad and the good in yourself, and readily work on the unresolved issues that are impeding your success, life gets better, easier and freer. Self-acceptance is a form of self-love, a process in which you are giving yourself the help, the time and the care to be the best version of yourself.

Self-Love is Honouring Yourself

Self-love means honouring your own needs in every aspect of your life; at work, in relationships, in accomplishments. If you can't love yourself first, you are not going to fully love someone or be fully accepting of any love you receive. Neither are you going to be in a healthy position to help or inspire others. Through sheer dint of willpower, you may be able to force yourself to, say, help others, but for genuine, heart-sourced, consistent and sustainable contributions and impact, you need to be powered by self-love.

A huge part of your success begins with getting a better sense and definition of yourself from the inside out. Self-love knows the aspects of self to celebrate and the aspects of self to change. It seeks to overcome self-defeating, self-sabotaging behaviours, and it knows how to claim empowerment. When you honour who you are, and when you embrace it, you are doing something revolutionary. You are committing to your vision of yourself as a success. When you do, you'll see before you a shining new path on which you can make huge strides towards an authentic, vibrant and powerful life.

Sharing Your Gifts

Each of us is on this earth for a reason, and an essential part of our journey is to uncover our life's purpose. Your calling brings meaning to your days. It calls to the best of you and you thrive when you have defined the reason for your existence. Without that lodestone, you may feel rudderless and lost. When you are questing for the meaning to your life, there may be times when you turn to self-destructive behaviours to fill the emptiness that arises from not knowing what you are meant to do.

There are no guidebooks, no formulas to tell you how to arrive at your greater calling. There is no lightning strike, no big boom of a thunderclap but, as we mentioned before, the universe does provide clues and tips to guide you on your journey.

It's simple. Think about peak experiences you've had, those best times of your life when you felt fully alive, joyful and delighted. Those experiences provide inklings of what your greater purpose may be.

For Angie, the answers came in the form of an old out-of-tune piano in a seniors' home. There has never been a question as to how important music is to Angie. She has a passion for the piano, a passion that has carried her through 10 years of disciplined study to emerge with 2 diplomas in piano performance. Nonetheless, she was unaware that her music would impact large numbers of people.

At 16, Angie was a frequent volunteer in a seniors' home. One day, she spotted a piano in the corner of a dining area. It didn't shine or gleam like the grand pianos that are primed for concert recitals and, to be honest, it was overlooked and neglected by the residents of the home. Nonetheless, Angie was drawn towards it. The keys were out of tune but her love for music won the day, and Angie played Fantasie Impromptu, one of Chopin's most haunting and beautiful pieces with many cross-rhythms. As her hands slid over the keys, firstly in *allegro agitato*, then changing to *largo* and *moderato cantabile*, Angie didn't notice she had an audience. As the last notes drifted into the air, Angie looked up. A lady in her 80s, a resident of the home, had come up to her. With tears streaming down her face, she said to Angie, "Thank you, that was beautiful."

Just like that, by following her passion and her heart, Angie realized that her purpose rested in making other people feel good, by bringing joy and beauty into their lives.

Going For Your Top Game

Making divine music has always been Sim's gift.

At the young age of 5, Sim's parents found her drumming on anything and everything, toy drums, ice-cream buckets, table tops. Her kindergarten teacher would attempt to deter Sim from playing beats with her hands on the school desk, but Sim never stopped. She was brimming over with energy, marching to the drumming of the music in her head.

This energy found expression at the Sikh temple service, during which Sim would be entranced by the sacred tabla drumming. Tabla is a set of 2 drums that is played by both hands, and is the most important and most popular percussion instrument in India. The pulsating rhythm, the quickening of the drums and the hypnotic beats made her very happy, and spoke to a passion within her to produce such sounds and beats.

Sim didn't care that she never saw any other girls or women playing the tabla. It didn't faze her that to be a professional tabla player required training by a Tabla Master. Instead, she taught herself. She observed and concentrated on replicating the beats that she heard and saw and, before too long, she created her own rhythm in time to the inner music that was playing inside her. Her musical gifts made her a cherished, special child.

One of the happiest days of her young life came when she received a set of tabla drums as a gift. Suddenly, she could give free rein to the music in her head, and she went after it with ferocity and determination. The music flowed through her and, despite lacking in formal training, she was soon invited to play the tabla at religious gatherings. It must have felt weird, from time to time, to be the only kid, and a girl at that, among the male adult players, but creating the sacred sounds in harmony was what truly mattered.

Though her parents were thrilled by her talent, not everyone was. Once, a man at a temple service objected to her presence on the stage because female tabla players were unheard of. He argued for her removal from the stage. To this day, Sim isn't sure what would have happened if her father hadn't spoken up. In no uncertain terms, her father overrode the stranger's objections by insisting that his daughter was going to stay right where she was. Sim continued playing.

By following her heart, Sim learned a valuable life experience, which was to always embrace yourself and to go for what you want, regardless of what convention or the rest of society may be wanting for you. Loving tabla as she did, Sim practiced exhaustively as a kid, when her peers were out having fun on the playground. Being a female in a field dominated by men threw a few challenges in her path. But it developed a strong sense of self, and it gave her an unerring compass on how and in which direction she should move forward.

That's how you get to your top game. If you want something, you need to be the one who pursues it. No one else will. Rather than depending on or needing to trawl through conflicting opinions from outsiders about what should be important to you, rely on your own sense, your own passion, and your heart to guide you towards what's meaningful.

Shifting to Clarity

In a world where change is a constant, how do you manage the rocking of the waves? What can you do to achieve clarity when you don't know which foot to put forward and in which direction?

Very simply, accept that clarity comes from within you. Once again, it doesn't come from outside of you. It may happen in a moment or from a series of decisions but it starts with you deciding to be clear in your purpose. There are steps that you can take in any situation so that you will be clearer tomorrow than you are today.

Recognize that clarity comes from managing your intentions and your expenditure of energy. Are you hanging out with people who are without aim in their lives, or are you connecting with those who are focused on their goals? Are you working and living in alignment with your own values? Are you deciding to shed those activities that don't serve your greater purpose? Are you indulging in time wasters like watching too much television, or are you actively immersing yourself in a variety of experiences to see if any of them resonate with you? For example, volunteering with different types of organizations may give you insight into which activities resonate more strongly with you.

Clarity does not come to you without any action being taken. As Joel A. Barker once said, *"Vision without action is merely a dream. Action without vision just passes the time. Vision with action can change the world."* By now, we hope that you understand that you have the power within you to change your world. Be mindful of where you are in your life now, and create a plan of action that will improve and take you one step outside of your situation. Soon, clarity will come to you and will assist in helping you find your own passion and calling in life.

A Masterpiece in Progress

Love all your flaws and imperfections as much as you do your strengths and talents. All these make up the warp and weft of the masterpiece that is You, because there isn't another person in the world who can do what you are capable of. For example, there are many gifted singers in the world, but each one delivers with a different pitch, a different nuance in voice and tone and emotions.

At the same time, clarity can come to you only when you keep challenging yourself, when you keep pushing your boundaries. As Fred Devito said, "If it doesn't challenge you, it doesn't change you." You don't know what you are capable of until you attempt something. Plan your next steps and work your plan. Push yourself off the edge of the pool and jump in!

Understand too that you are constantly changing. Each experience you undergo shapes and molds you, it adds depth and dimension, it refines your purpose and it distills your sense of purpose until it is a finely edged instrument. Accept that the destination is not the purpose, it's the journey. Every day of your life, you are a work in progress, and that's okay.

Some people see the world as being filled with problems and danger. Others see the world as being filled with unlimited promise and possibilities. All it takes is a mindset-shift. That pivotal and crucial mindset-shift happens by asking yourself this question:

What would you do now if you knew that you could not fail?

* * *

Success Story from the Frontlines #6: Karrie Tam
Music Educator

"I will NEVER be a piano teacher!" was what I said one day while having a heated argument with my mom when I was 13 years old. My mom wanted me to quit my ballet lessons for my piano studies. I never would have guessed then that teaching piano was what I would have a talent and a passion for now.

I am a perfectionist and I had set goals very early on in my life. I wanted to study at an Ivy League university, become a criminal lawyer, marry the man of my dreams and have a couple of beautiful children. Although I didn't become a lawyer, I am very grateful for the life that I have with my wonderful family of 5.

To me, success doesn't mean to be rich and famous. I feel thankful and successful because I am able to live my passion and hobby in the form of my piano teaching career. Thirteen years ago, my husband and I made a difficult decision to move from Canada to Hong Kong in pursuit of achieving our dreams. We have achieved a lot and we are glad we made some good choices along the way.

It's been 25 years and I still fill my days with piano lessons with my students because I love to see how a child develops and unfolds her musical talent week after week, how they get recognized at piano competitions, and how proud they become when they receive their examination score. I take pride in inspiring my piano students, their parents and fellow piano teachers on my philosophy of teaching through positive encouragement and motivation, to make piano lessons more exciting.

I owned an artist agency that represented reputable musicians to perform in concerts and recitals in Asia. It wasn't a profitable business for 7 years, and I had my fair share of struggles due to my inexperience, especially in the early years, where money was lost, legal issues came up, and relationships with some respectable musicians were tarnished. Despite the challenges, I loved every moment of it because it taught me so much about the music business. When mistakes were made, I was always conscious of learning from each one so as to never repeat them again.

Although I can say that I have earned a lot of respect in my community over the years, it isn't easy to stay at the top of my teaching. In order to thrive, I am always upgrading myself with further studies and readings. I stay in touch with the teaching community and music industry to learn about new technology, new products, new books, new syllabi, concerts, and competitions.

Today, I spend much time still teaching and giving master classes, and adjudicating in competitions and festivals. I recently finished editing 3 beautiful piano books in celebration of the 90th anniversary of Disney, that were published by New Century Music. I have co-founded a music competition that is held annually called "Hong Kong Students Open Music Competition" because I noticed there was no platform for students to compete in a positive and encouraging atmosphere in Hong Kong. I am proud to say that our competition is now in its 7th successful year!

No matter how busy we get, no matter how advanced technology gets, we must include music in our lives. To be successful in life, you have to work hard, and play hard. You also have to love doing what you do best. When you keep living your passion, more doors will open for you than you can ever imagine.

Chapter 10
Brick by Brick

Our deepest fear is not that we are inadequate.
Our deepest fear is that we are powerful beyond measure.
It is our light, not our darkness that most frightens us.
We ask ourselves, 'Who am I to be brilliant, gorgeous, talented,
fabulous?' Actually, who are you not to be?

– Marianne Williamson

Throughout this book, we have spoken in a collective voice. As friends and business partners, we have many, many ideas, values and principles in common, and yet we couldn't be more different from each other. As such, we thought in the final chapter in our book to speak to you individually. As if we were having a fireside chat, a time of sharing between good friends.

Before we get into that, we want to share a piece of our explanatory statement that appears on our website of our networking group, WIISE (Women Inspiring Innovative Successful Entrepreneurs) Women's Network, as to how it is we came up with the book title, *Define and Defy: Unleashing Your Inner Potential.*

"Everyone goes through life trying to find meaning and purpose. We begin to *define* ourselves through various experiences and lessons we go through. Everything that happens in our life comprises who we are on an intrapersonal level, including our passions, goals and vocation. When we have an understanding of who we are, we move on to the next level, that which is the interpersonal level. How we fit into the community, and what kind of mark we want to leave in this world is related to how we challenge and *defy* the status quo and what society deems to be normal and possible.

We all have the power to create what we want most. Although nothing worthwhile will ever come easy, once you have a vision and an understanding of who you are and what you want to accomplish in your life, you will unlock your true potential to do great things."

Laying the Foundation One Day at a Time

No house is built in a single day. It is constructed brick by brick with precise skill which takes years to master. The bricks have to be laid in a visually-appealing way, the mortar that sticks the bricks together has to be of the right consistency. Too thick and it impedes the rest of the construction, too thin and the structure is at risk of collapse. When it comes to the odd corner, the bricklayer has to use his tools, be it a trowel, a brick-cutter or a chisel, to shape the brick to fit.

We are the architects and the bricklayers of our own lives. Unlike the Greek goddess of war, intellect, wisdom and the arts, Athena, who was born fully formed and fully armoured out of the head of Zeus, we are born into the world naked. We design our lives with our choices, some of which don't bear fruit until several years later.

Every day brings us a fresh promise. How does each of us employ this promise and potential? It all starts with one step, one step towards recognizing that we are filled with untold possibility, to create lives that create positive ripples around the world. It starts with one brick, then another, to lay the foundation from which we can springboard into action. Every day, we should move into the kind of action that will take us one step beyond where we were the day before. It was Mikhail Gorbachev, former Soviet Union President, who, speaking at Harvard in 2007 said, "If you don't move forward, sooner or later you begin to move backward."

Great leaders have shared this view. Abraham Lincoln said "I am a slow walker, but I never walk back." Carl Sandburg, American poet and writer, has been quoted as saying, "I don't know where I'm going, but I'm on my way." Polish activist Rosa Luxemburg said, "Those who do not move, do not notice their chains."

Designing your life is an unending work-in-progress. Mary Catherine Bateson said it best in "Composing a Life" when she wrote, "Composing a life involves a continual reimagining of the future and reinterpretation of the past to give meaning to the present, remembering best those events that prefigured what followed, forgetting those that proved to have no meaning within the narrative."

Moving and getting ahead requires focus and courage, but it is not based on just one act or pursuit. Forward movement involves a quilt of activities, a variety of routines or endeavours including networking, expanding your knowledge base through reading and education, experimenting and constantly pushing yourself beyond your boundaries, taking stock, dreaming new dreams or dusting off old ones. Very likely, you have a multiplicity of life-purposes which, when fulfilled, add value to your life and heighten the meaning of what it is to be human.

The purpose of sharing our strategies to success is not to insist that you adopt our habits. Rather, we offer them in the spirit of collaboration, and if by doing so, we inspire someone to live a bigger life, we will have achieved the goals of our book. In each of the next sections, we will speak of our individual pursuits, habits of choice, and pass along some snippets of wisdom. Along our journeys to this juncture, we were at some point influenced by guides and mentors, and it is in tribute to them that we share our experiences with you on the following:

- What we do to get ahead
- Strengthening the foundation
- All experiences are worthwhile

What We Do to Get Ahead

Angie:

I read real estate books and magazines to keep my finger on the industry's pulse, I load up on self-development books and I listen to audio recordings at work and in my car. That way, I don't begrudge the time spent commuting and am in fact enriching my mind while behind the wheel. I drive an average of 2 hours a day, 6 days a week for work and business; by gainfully employing the commuting time, I am gaining an extra half day of inspiring and motivating messages every week. We are given the gift of time, freely, and it's up to us to maximize its use or to squander it away. By the way, occasionally, I switch the car radio to calming piano classics because music stirs and elevates my soul, and it keeps me grounded and in tune with my inner being.

Sim:

I am committed to the study of success. I am curious about the things that successful people do to get to where they are, and how they live their lives. It doesn't matter to me if they flaunt their riches in a garage full of Bentleys and Rolls-Royces or paper their bathrooms with gold. What I am intrigued by is how a person gets started and stays on the road to success. Business and entrepreneurship runs in my blood. When I started my business from scratch, I couldn't fathom how successful I would be. Sure, I've had my fair share of mistakes and setbacks, but I came to appreciate that there is an upside to disappointments. As I am a visual learner, I prefer watching videos that chart the successes of business entrepreneurs as well as those who have encountered big wins and big losses like bankruptcy. I also enjoy meeting successful entrepreneurs and learning from the best.

Strengthening the Foundation

Your life is a puzzle of many pieces. Sometimes you know where the pieces fit, and at other times you are stuck with an awkward fragment that defies explanation. Sometimes, opportunities come disguised as disappointments but, if you look beyond the pain and understand the lesson, your setback becomes a breakthrough. Timing is a big part of success but preparation is just as key. As we gained more experience in business through the years, we acquired confidence to branch into other investments. The result is that we are creating multiple streams of income that allow us to leverage our time and our resources, which has allowed us to work hard and play harder! Our multiple streams of income make up the ace in our pocket. Our families have shaped much of our inner foundations for success, whether they did so consciously or unconsciously.

Angie:

My parents stressed the importance of smart financial investments in real estate, mutual funds, transportation and other wealth-building assets. When I was young, I was fascinated with collecting and saving money. During Chinese New Year, my birthday, and other special events, it is the tradition for our parents and older relatives to give red pockets filled with money to young kids. My parents collected my monetary gifts and started a bank account for me, distilling in me at a very young age the good habit of thrift and savings. Additionally, I've observed through the years that most of my friends and relatives, who are tied to a job, are in effect swapping their time for money. They are time-starved and I decided at a very young age that I wasn't going to follow in their footsteps.

Sim:

My parents had no notion about savings. They made money, spent money and lost money. For them, it was rags to riches and back to rags again. They didn't pass on any lessons or habits on savings to us. But when I started managing my own finances at 19 years of age, I quickly became money-smart. I took full responsibility for my financial health, carefully measured risks and rewards before making investments and was a good steward of the financial wealth I had acquired. Supported by healthy financial habits, I built a company from the ground up from zero to multi-millions in revenues in only 3 years.

All Experiences are Worthwhile

There are no mistakes or failures. It's how you react to a situation or a problem that determines whether it's a crippling setback or a gift. It's not easy to see any disappointment as a precious gift because often our ego gets in the way. The inner critic pops up and blames us for investing precious time in a wrong venture. But what if you viewed the letdown as preparing you for something even better? You may not know what that something better is at this moment, but when you assume the mindset of a "winner" rather than a "loser," you are already ahead of the game.

When the universe serves up what you think is a challenge, you may be tempted to have a hissy fit or sulk and ruin the rest of your day. Disappointments are signposts to guide you down a different way; instead of bewailing, "Why me?" ask instead, "What can I learn from this?"

Brazilian author Paulo Coelho phrased it so elegantly in *The Devil and Miss Prym* when he wrote, "When we least expect it, life sets us a challenge to test our courage and willingness to change; at such a moment, there is no point in pretending that nothing has happened or in saying that we are not yet ready. The challenge will not wait. Life does not look back. A week is more than enough time for us to decide whether or not to accept our destiny."

Angie:

Being used to success in academia and having planned out my life in a straight line from high school to an undergraduate degree, I wasn't prepared for the curve balls that life threw at me. At first, I struggled when the winds of change blew me off my feet, but I soon regained my balance and footing and discovered that my perspectives and attitudes had changed. I had a grander vision of possibility, I gained deep insights into myself and I made the precious discovery that, ultimately, what I think and choose to believe shapes my life. My life and mission started to become most clear and defined during my trying times. I can't fathom what I'd be doing right now if my life didn't go 'off course,' enabling me to think and look deeper towards my inner self.

When I recalibrated my life, all the childhood goals and dreams that had been suppressed came to life again. What a ride it has been! The desire that I had as a girl to positively impact people's lives has fully flowered. What you hold in your hand is a manifestation of that desire. This book has opened more doors than we had envisioned to reach out to hundreds and thousands and tens of thousands of people through public motivational speaking. It has given impetus and lent speed and commitment to starting our networking group WIISE (Women Inspiring Innovative Successful Entrepreneurs) Women's Network, so that we may motivate, encourage, inspire, cheer on and support each other in the pursuit of balanced, happy, successful and joyful lives.

Sim:

Never in my wildest dreams did I anticipate I would be at this point, telling my life story and positioned to inspire and motivate women. I have had my setbacks but none of them prevented me from moving forward. Four years ago, I was scraping the barrel and surviving off my student loans to make ends meet. It was a crucial juncture in my life because I made the conscious decision to keep doing positive things that would get me closer to my goal. Even when it seemed dark, I chose to remain positive. During those times, I viewed the smallest achievements as the biggest accomplishments. I was my own cheerleader and coach. I have never had any fear of the unknown. Life is a discovery, it's an exploration, it is an adventure. I've had one heck of a ride so far, and am leaning forward to embrace what is ahead.

One Chapter Ends, Another Begins

As our book comes to an end, we say to you, don't settle for less, don't settle for crumbs. Find out what's your inner truth, use your voice and speak up for yourself. When you learn to speak up for yourself, you will find yourself compelled to speak up for those who have yet to muster the courage to ask more for themselves. We are all connected; as we prosper and live fully, so do others. We have a responsibility to each other, to elevate ourselves and others so that we shall not just survive, but thrive in this world beaming with opportunities, love and excitement.

As this chapter in our lives comes to an end, we draw open the curtains on another, our networking group. Let us now introduce you to the WIISE Women's Network.

* * *

WIISE Women's Network

There is energy in community, there is strength in collaboration, there is power in finding your own tribe. There is safety in numbers, and there is creativity in diversity. There is vitality in a collective consciousness and there are precious stories and priceless wisdom to be shared among generations. We can be baby boomers, Gen X or Millennials; regardless of the labels, what we have in common is a desire to succeed in business and to share our knowledge, insights and understanding with the ones who come after us. There is no need to reinvent the wheel each and every time. There are certain steps to be followed in starting a new business and, if we can pool together our collective knowledge, we can shorten the gestation and start-up times and minimize birthing pains.

It's Angie again. When I first became an entrepreneur, I very quickly surmised that behind the fun excitement and the novelty of business building lay stress, anxiety and uncertainty. There was so much information to absorb and I was too new to the ropes to understand how to prioritize my time. Every small detail needed as much air-time as did the big issues. While having a mentor was great, I often wondered if there was a group of like-minded entrepreneurs I could tap into, a group with wide ranging experience, from newbies to business icons. When I met Sim, who became my guide and explorer-in-arms through the expanding business landscape, I wondered what if there was a Sim for every Angie who plans to go into business.

From that thought sprung the idea to create WIISE Women's Network. Our purpose is to provide an empowering yet safe environment, a motivation-galvanizing, respect-honouring space for like-minded women who want to lead a fully passionate, adventurous and authentic life.

We invite you to regard this as your "haven" as you are finding your way around the business landscape, where you can find answers and encouragement and a broad worldview. If you need extra motivation every so often, you'll find it here too. If you are already a model of business success, consider this a space where you can give back. And you may be delightfully and unexpectedly surprised that, as you mingle with the next generation of business leaders, your batteries get recharged, your perspectives are refreshed, and you may find new worlds and new lands to conquer. The world is evolving at a faster and faster rate, change is the constant and, to stay at the forefront, we have to give each other a helping hand.

For both of us, WIISE Women's Network is all about empowerment, nurturing and support. We may be a small voice at the moment but we know that from an acorn grows a mighty oak.

The time we've been given is a gift beyond measure, and it is up to us to be worthy of the gift, to not just go through the motions daily, but to live purposefully so that we may shine light in our corners of the world, wherever we may be. We welcome you to join us in living mindful, extraordinary lives that resonate with happiness and meaning.

All the best to your success.

Get involved with us on social media
Facebook: www.facebook.com/wiisewomensnetwork
Twitter: @WIISE_Women
LinkedIn: WIISE Women's Network
Instagram: WIISEWOMENSNETWORK
Blog: wiisewomensnetwork.wordpress.com

WIISE WOMEN'S NETWORK IS POWERED BY: